Mikhail and Vyacheslav Durnenkov

THE DRUNKS

translated by

NINA RAINE

from a literal translation by Maria Kozlovskaya

NICK HERN BOOKS

London

www.nickhernbooks.co.uk

ABOUT THE ROYAL SHAKESPEARE COMPANY

The Royal Shakespeare Company at Stratford-upon-Avon was formed in 1960 as a home for Shakespeare's plays, classics and new plays.

The first Artistic Director Peter Hall created an ensemble theatre company of mostly young actors and writers. The core of the work was Shakespeare, combined with a search for writers who were as true to their time as Shakespeare was to his. The Company was led by Hall, Peter Brook and Michel Saint-Denis. Hall's founding principles were threefold. He wanted the Company to embrace the freedom and power of Shakespeare's work, to train and develop young actors and directors and to experiment in new ways of making theatre. Rejecting dogma, he urged the Company in a 1963 address to "Keep open, keep critical... Our Company is young, we are searching, and whatever we find today, a new search will be necessary tomorrow."

The Company has had a distinct personality from the beginning. The search for new forms of writing and directing was led by Peter Brook. He pushed writers to experiment. "Just as Picasso set out to capture a larger slice of the truth by painting a face with several eyes and noses, Shakespeare, knowing that man is living his everyday life and at the same time is living intensely in the invisible world of his thoughts and feelings, developed a method through which we can see at one and the same time the look on a man's face and the vibrations of his brain."

A rich and varied range of writers flowed into the Company and have continued to do so with the RSC's renewed commitment in placing living dramatists at the heart of the Company. These include: Harold Pinter, Howard Barker, Edward Bond, Howard Brenton, Edward Albee, David Edgar, Peter Flannery, Martin Crimp, Caryl Churchill, Tony Harrison, Wole Soyinka, Stephen Poliakoff, Tom Stoppard, Timberlake Wertenbaker, Martin McDonagh, Marina Carr, debbie tucker green, David Greig, Rona Munro, Adriano Shaplin, Roy Williams and Anthony Neilson.

Alongside the Royal Shakespeare Theatre, The Other Place was established in 1975. The 400-seat Swan Theatre was added in 1986. The RSC's spaces have seen some of the most epic, challenging and era-defining theatre – Peter Brook's Beckettian *King Lear* with Paul Scofield in the title role, Charles Marowitz's *Theatre of Cruelty* season which premiered Peter Weiss' *Marat/Sade*, Trevor Nunn's studio *Macbeth*, Michael Boyd's restoration of ensemble with *The Histories Cycle* and David Greig and Roy Williams' searing war plays *The American Pilot* and *Days of Significance*.

The Company today is led by Michael Boyd, who is taking the Company's founding ideals forward. His belief in ensemble theatre making, internationalism, in new work and active approaches to Shakespeare in the classroom has inspired the Company to landmark projects such as *The Complete Works Festival, Stand up for Shakespeare* and *The Histories Cycle*. He is overseeing the transformation of our theatres which will welcome the world's theatre artists onto our stages to celebrate the power and freedom of Shakespeare's work and the wealth of inspiration it offers to living playwrights.

The Drunks is generously supported by
THE LECHE TRUST

The RSC Ensemble is generously supported by
THE GATSBY CHARITABLE FOUNDATION and THE KOVNER FOUNDATION

The RSC Literary Department is generously supported by THE DRUE HEINZ TRUST

The RSC's New Work is generously supported by
CHRISTOPHER SETON ABELE on behalf of THE ARGOSY FOUNDATION

The RSC is grateful for the significant support of its principal funder,
Arts Council England, without which our work would not be possible.
Around 50 per cent of the RSC's income is self-generated from Box Office sales,
sponsorship, donations, enterprise and partnerships with other organisations.

ARTS COUNCIL ENGLAND

REVOLUTIONS

This August, the RSC launches a four year celebration and exploration of theatre in Russia and the former Soviet Union. We begin with the première of two new RSC commissioned plays from Russia and Ukraine, performed by the RSC Ensemble. *The Grain Store* by Natal'ia Vorozhbit and *The Drunks* by Mikhail and Vyacheslav Durnenkov capture the voices of an exciting new generation of post-Soviet playwrights. *Revolutions* will culminate in a major Russian contribution to our 2012 Olympic celebration.

For over a century, Russian theatre has had a profound influence on theatre in the West and particularly that of the RSC. After Shakespeare, Chekhov is the most performed playwright in the world and Russian work has always featured heavily in the RSC's repertoire. Stanislavski began and is still at the heart of Western film and theatre practice. The RSC has broken free of this by also embracing the bold, expressive style championed by Stanislavski's rebellious pupil, Meyerhold, especially in Peter Brook's *A Midsummer Night's Dream*, Trevor Nunn's *Nicholas Nickleby* and Michael Boyd's *The Histories*.

We open *Revolutions* with our new plays. These plays are the first fruits of an adventure which began back in 2005. We are proud to be working with Associate Director International at the Royal Court, Elyse Dodgson, who was invited to join the RSC as consultant by our then Associate Director, Dominic Cooke. Dominic, Elyse and RSC Company Dramaturg Jeanie O'Hare went to Moscow to work with nine writers selected by Elyse from the emerging writers of Russia and Ukraine. Giving them stimuli from the classics while encouraging them to engage with contemporary Russian society, we gave the writers seed commissions. Of those nine, three were strong enough to become full commissions and two are now on our main stage. This development of international work is central to Michael Boyd's vision at the RSC and further projects are planned. We are delighted that in this case the searching intelligence of the Royal Court's international programme has been the key to unlocking a generation of writers who are hungry to write for large stages.

This production of *The Drunks* was first performed by the Royal Shakespeare Company at The Courtyard Theatre, Stratford-upon-Avon, on 21 August 2009.

The cast was as follows:

CONDUCTOR / 3rd ILYA	**Charles Aitken**
1st SUBORDINATE / 2nd POLICEMAN / 2nd ILYA	**Adam Burton**
RAILWAY WORKER / VASSILIEV	**David Carr**
MAYOR	**Brian Doherty**
KOTOMTSEV	**Darrell D'Silva**
SCENE ANNOUNCER / 1st ILYA	**Dyfan Dwyfor**
2nd BABITSKY / SAVELIEV	**Phillip Edgerley**
MAYOR'S AIDE (KOSTYA)	**Christine Entwisle**
PASSENGER / ELDERLY MAN	**James Gale**
3rd PASSENGER / 2nd BARFLY	**Paul Hamilton**
2nd SUBORDINATE / MAN IN HAT	**James Howard**
SERGEY	**Richard Katz**
BABITSKY	**Sandy Neilson**
ILYA	**Jonjo O'Neill**
YOUNG KOSTYA / 1st BARFLY	**Peter Peverley**
PLUMP WOMAN / WOMAN IN BERET	**Sophie Russell**
3rd BABITSKY / 1st POLICEMAN	**Clarence Smith**
2nd PASSENGER / EFREMOV	**James Traherne**
NATASHA	**Hannah Young**

All other parts played by members of the company.

The running time is approximately 1 hour and 40 minutes in length. There is no interval.

Directed by	**Anthony Neilson**
Designed by	**Tom Piper**
Lighting designed by	**Oliver Fenwick**
Music and Sound designed by	**Nick Powell**
Movement by	**Anna Morrissey**
Company Dramaturg	**Jeanie O'Hare**
Company text and voice work by	**Alison Bomber and Tess Dignan**
Fights by	**Terry King**
Assistant Director	**Helen Leblique**
Music Director	**Michael Cryne**
Casting by	**Hannah Miller** CDG
Production Manager	**Mark Graham**
Costume Supervisor	**Bushy Westfallen**
Assistant Costume Supervisor	**Gayle Woodsend**
Company Manager	**Michael Dembowicz**
Stage Manager	**Pip Horobin**
Deputy Stage Manager	**Gabrielle Sanders**
Assistant Stage Manager	**Amy Griffin**

MUSICIANS

Guitar/Balalaika/Ukelele	**Nicholas Lee**
Saw/Violin	**Jeff Moore**
Flutes	**Ian Reynolds**
Trumpet	**Chris Seddon**
Horn	**David Statham**
Trombone	**Kevin Pitt**
Percussion	**James Jones**
Keyboards	**Michael Cryne**

EMBEDDED WRITERS AT THE RSC

The potential for new work at the RSC is something we take very seriously. Our embedded writer policy is just one of a raft of strategies designed to inspire playwrights.

We believe that a writer embedded with our actors helps establish a creative culture within the Company which both inspires new work and creates an ever more urgent sense of enquiry into the classics. The benefits work both ways. Actors naturally learn the language of dramaturgical intervention and sharpen their interpretation of roles. Writers benefit from re-discovering the stagecraft and theatre skills that have been lost over time. They regain the knack of writing roles for leading actors. They become hungry to put death, beauty and metaphor back on stage.

As part of this strategy we have played host to key international writers for the last three years. Tarell McCraney is our current RSC/CAPITAL Centre International Playwright in Residence. He works in the rehearsal room with the Ensemble Company on our Shakespeare productions. Whilst contributing creatively to the work of the directors and actors he is also developing his own writing and theatre practice. His new play for the RSC will be performed by this current Ensemble in 2011. His post is funded by the CAPITAL Centre at Warwick University where he teaches as part of his residency.

Tarell follows on from Adriano Shaplin who was with the RSC from 2006-8.

We also invite British writers to spend time with us in the rehearsal room and contribute dramaturgically to both our main stage Shakespeares and our Young People's Shakespeare. There is a generation of playwrights who are ready to write their career-defining work. We are creating conditions at the heart of the RSC in which this generation can take themselves seriously as dramatists and thrive.

Special thanks go to Elyse Dodgson, Dominic Cooke, Noah Birksted-Breen and everyone who helped with our Moscow workshops; Tanya Oskolkova, Vladimir Fleisher, Igor Troilin and all the staff at Meyerhold Theatre Center; Elena Kovalskaya at Lubimovka Young Playwrights Festival; and Elena Gremina at Theatre.Doc.

THE COMPANY

CHARLES **AITKEN**

ADAM **BURTON**

DAVID **CARR**

CONDUCTOR/ 3ᴿᴰ ILYA
RSC DEBUT SEASON:
Oliver in *As You Like It*,
Conductor/3rd Ilya in
The Drunks.
trained: RADA.
theatre includes: *Othello*
(Frantic Assembly/Lyric
Hammersmith/tour);
The Taming of the Shrew
(Wilton's Music Hall);
Midnight Cowboy (Assembly
Rooms, Edinburgh); *Paradise
Lost* (Headlong); *Hair* (Gate);
London Assurance (Royal
Exchange).
television: *Bonkers*.
film: *Love Nest* (short).

1ˢᵀ SUBORDINATE/ 2ᴺᴰ POLICEMAN/ 2ᴺᴰ ILYA
RSC DEBUT SEASON:
Sicilian Lord in *The Winter's
Tale*, Metellus Cimber/
Titinius in *Julius Caesar*, 1st
Subordinate/2nd Policeman
/2nd Ilya in *The Drunks*.
trained: LIPA.
theatre includes: *Timon of
Athens, A Midsummer Night's
Dream* (Shakespeare's Globe);
*Masque of the Red Death,
Faust* (Punchdrunk); *As You
Like It* (Derby Playhouse);
Baggage (Pleasance); *The
Adding Machine* (Rogue State/
Courtyard); *The Waiting Game*
(Courtyard/King's Head); *Heart
of a Dog* (Rogue State/Assembly
Rooms); *Blood Brothers* (No.1
tour); *Gogol's Underdogs*
(Rogue State/The Underbelly).
television includes: *Doctors,
Jekyll, Casualty, Harry on the
Boat, Dangerfield, Treflan* (Welsh
BAFTA winner).
film includes: *The Butcher's
Shop* (Open Award winner at
Venice Film Festival), *Short/
Film* (best short film nomination
at Austin Film Festival), *Breaker*
(best short film nomination at
Golden Lion Film Festival).

RAILWAY WORKER/ VASSILIEV
RSC DEBUT SEASON:
Charles in *As You Like It*,
Egeon in *The Comedy of
Errors*, Railway Worker/
Vassiliev in *The Drunks*.
trained: Central School of
Speech and Drama.
theatre includes: *King
Lear, Original Sin* (Sheffield
Crucible); *Antony and
Cleopatra, 48-98, Brother to
Brother* (Talawa Theatre Co.);
*Macbeth, Deadmeat, The
Comedy of Errors, Two Tracks
and Text Me* (West Yorkshire
Playhouse); *One Flew Over
the Cuckoo's Nest* (New Vic);
Futurology (Suspect Culture/
Scottish National Theatre);
Romeo and Juliet (USA tour).
television includes: *The
Bill, A Touch of Frost, Soldier
Soldier, Casualty, The Family
Man, Living It, Doctors*.
film: *Green Street*.
radio includes: *Beau
Carnival, Freefall, Speaking in
Tongues*.

MICHAEL CRYNE
MUSIC DIRECTOR

RSC: As Music Director and Supervisor: *As You Like It, Othello, The Tragedy of Thomas Hobbes, The Penelopiad.*
this season: *The Drunks.*
trained: Michael studied composition at the Guildhall School of Music and Drama and at the London College of Music.
recent works include: *4 Spanish Dances* for Brass quintet; a cycle of Edgar Allan Poe poems for tenor and piano; *Between Scylla and Charybdis*, a piece commissioned and performed by the RSC in October 2008.
previous notable works include: *White Smoke*, a concerto for alto saxophone; *Chelinot*, a music-theatre work (The Times Critics Choice, Summer 2006).
other credits include: *Ella, Meet Marilyn* (Theatre Royal, Stratford East); *Side by Side by Sondheim* (Union Theatre); *West Side Story* (Warwick Arts Centre).

ELYSE DODGSON
INTERNATIONAL CONSULTANT

Elyse has been on the artistic team of the Royal Court Theatre since 1985, first as Director of the Young People's Theatre and from 1996 as Associate Director, Head of International Department.

She has led play development programmes for emerging playwrights in all parts of the world and produced dozens of plays in International Playwrights Seasons at the Royal Court for more than a decade. She is the founder and director of the Royal Court International Residency which began in 1989 and continues to bring international playwrights to London every summer. She began working with Russian language playwrights in 1999 and has produced work by Vassily Sigarev, The Presnyakov Brothers and Natal'ia Vorozhbit at the Royal Court.

BRIAN DOHERTY

MAYOR

RSC: *God in Ruins* (RSC/ Soho), *Macbeth, Macbett, Great Expectations.*
this season: Autolycus in *The Winter's Tale*, Decius Brutus/Poet in *Julius Caesar*, Mayor in *The Drunks.*
theatre includes: *Three Sisters, Down the Line, Translations, Tarry Flynn, The Murphy Initiative* (Abbey); *Aristocrats* (National Theatre); *Stones in his Pockets* (Duke of York's); *All in the Head, The Crucible, Happy Birthday Dear Alice, The Glass Menagerie, Observe the Sons of Ulster Marching Towards the Somme* (Red Kettle); *Pentecost, Boomtown, School for Scandal* (Rough Magic); *Car Show (Love Me)* (Corn Exchange); *Romantic Friction* (Read Co.); *Emma* (Storytellers); *Zoe's Play* (The Ark); *Amphibians* (Tin Drum); *Studs* (Passion Machine); *Conquest of the South Pole* (Theatre Demo).
film and television includes: *Billy the Kid, Pure Mule, Casualty, Doctors, Fair City, The Clinic, Glenroe, Perrier's Bounty, Garage.*

DARRELL D'SILVA

KOTOMTSEV

RSC: *Hecuba, A Midsummer Night's Dream, A Month in the Country, Troilus and Cressida, Camino Real, Spanish Tragedy, Henry VIII, Doctor Faustus.*
this season: Polixenes in *The Winter's Tale*, Mark Antony in *Julius Caesar*, Kotomtsev in *The Drunks*.
trained: Drama Centre, London.
theatre includes: *The White Devil* (Menier Chocolate Factory); *Fall* (Traverse); *The Rose Tattoo, Royal Hunt of the Sun, Tales from Vienna Woods, Closer, Further than the Furthest Thing* (National Theatre); *Clouds* (No.1 tour); *Paradise Lost* (Northampton); *Absolutely! (Perhaps)* (Wyndham's); *The Lying Kind* (Royal Court); *Antarctica* (Savoy); *Six Characters Looking for an Author* (Young Vic); *Tear from a Glass Eye* (Gate); *Chasing the Moment* (One Tree); *Romeo and Juliet, The Three Musketeers* (Sheffield Crucible).

television includes: *Trial and Retribution, Bonekickers, Criminal Justice, Poppy Shakespeare, Saddam's Tribe, The First New Heart, Krakatoa – The Last Days, Eleventh Hour, Spooks, Lawless, Messiah 3, Prime Suspect, Out of the Blue, Cambridge Spies.*
film: *Dirty Pretty Things.*

MIKHAIL DURNENKOV CO-WRITER
RSC DEBUT SEASON: *The Drunks.*
Mikhail was born in 1978 in the town of Tynda in the Amur Region, and worked as a watchman, metal worker, director, actor, engineer, TV journalist and TV presenter. He is presently a playwright and script writer. Mikhail has written over 15 plays and film scripts and, since 2001, has been a regular participant in the new writing festivals May Readings, Lubimovka and New Drama.
produced plays include: *Cultural Layer* (Young People's Theatre, Tver/ Golosova 20 Theatre Centre, Togliatti); *The Blue Metal Worker* (Winner of the Debut Prize of the October Literary Magazine. Theatre. Doc, Moscow); *Crossing Project* (Teatrarium Theatre, Moscow); *The Red Cup* (Praktika Theatre, Moscow); *The Last Summer Day* (Moscow Art Theatre); *The Last Rehearsal Project* (Golosova 20 Theatre Centre, Togliatti).

VYACHESLAV DURNENKOV CO-WRITER
RSC DEBUT SEASON: *The Drunks.*
Vyacheslav has written 20 plays, some of which have been co-written with his brother Mikhail. His plays have been produced at the Moscow Art Theatre, Practica and Yermolova Theatres (Moscow), Voronezh Chamber Theatre and Globus (Novosibirsk), among others. His plays have been published in the magazines *Theatre, Contemporary Playwriting, Art of Film* and *Cultural Layer Collection of Plays*. He has won of a number of awards for his plays including Best Play at the Russian New Drama Festival in 2005 and 2008.
Vyacheslav is also actively involved in the international educational playwriting project, Class Act, in association with the Traverse Theatre and British Council in Russia, which inspires school pupils to write stage plays for the first time. Vyacheslav is currently writing projects for film and television. He is married with three children and lives and works in Togliatti.

DYFAN DWYFOR

SCENE ANNOUNCER/ 1ˢᵀ ILYA

RSC DEBUT SEASON:
William in *As You Like It*, Dromio of Ephesus in *The Comedy of Errors*, Scene Announcer/1st Ilya in *The Drunks*.

trained: Royal Welsh College of Music and Drama.

theatre includes: *Six Characters in Search of an Author* (Chichester/West End); *Hamlet* (National Youth Theatre of Wales).

theatre whilst training includes: *The Comedy of Errors* (for RSC Complete Works Festival), *The Winter's Tale*, *Twelfth Night*, *Gas*, *Take Me, Somewhere*, *Quadrophenia*.

television includes: *Caerdydd, Rownd & Rownd, Pen Tennyn, A470*.

film includes: *I Know You Know, The Baker, Oed yr Addewid*.

PHILLIP EDGERLEY

2ᴺᴰ BABITSKY/ SAVELIEV

RSC: *Two Gentlemen of Verona, Julius Caesar*.

this season: Cleomenes in *The Winter's Tale*, Flavius/ Popilius/Antony's Servant/ Volumnius in *Julius Caesar*, 2nd Babitsky/ Saveliev in *The Drunks*.

trained: The London Centre for Theatre Studies, The Actors Company.

theatre includes: *Gone Too Far* (Royal Court); *Some Kinda Arizona* (Croydon Warehouse); *Julius Caesar* (Lyric Hammersmith); *Duck Variations, Kiss of the Spiderwoman, Mary Stuart, Hamlet* (Nuffield); *Much Ado about Nothing, Dr Faustus* (Oxford Shakespeare Co.); *Luther* (National Theatre); *A Day Well Spent, On the Razzle* (Chichester Festival); *A Bed Full of Foreigners* (Theatre Royal); *Dancing at Lughnasa, Been so Long* (Jermyn Street); *Another Country* (Brockley Jack Theatre); *Bookworms, The Crucible, King Lear* (Fringe).

television includes: *Doctors, Life As We Know It, EastEnders, Footballers' Wives, Ultimate Force, The Bill*.

film includes: *Dead Rich, Chicane*.

radio includes: *Bernice Summerfield - The Empire State, Doctor Who*.

CHRISTINE ENTWISLE

MAYOR'S AIDE (KOSTYA)

RSC DEBUT SEASON:
Phoebe in *As You Like It*, Adriana in *The Comedy of Errors*, Mayor's Aide (Kostya) in *The Drunks*.

theatre includes: *Six Characters in Search of an Author* (Gielgud/Headlong/ Chichester); *Half Life* (National Theatre of Scotland); *The Wonderful World of Dissocia* (Royal Court/National Theatre of Scotland); *Duckie, C'est Vauxhall* (Barbican); *Vassa* (Almeida/Albery); *A Family Affair* (Theatr Clwyd); *Wonderhorse* (Edinburgh Festival/ICA/BAC); *Edward Gant* (Theatre Royal, Plymouth); *I Am Dandy* (Purcell Rooms/BAC); *Ubu*

Kunst, Missing Jesus, Fine (Young Vic); *People Shows 100-103* (International tour); *The Wedding, Paper Walls* (Scarlet Theatre).
television and film includes: *Attachments, Holby City, Mothers and Daughters, At Dawning, A&E, Where the Heart Is, Dalziel and Pascoe, Storm Damages, Deeper Still.*
radio: *Heredity.*
writing includes: *Wonder Horse* (ongoing); *Bat Boy, Death of a Double Act* (North West Vision and Media, UK Film Council); *Missing Jesus, Fine, Perilous Stuff* (Young Vic); *Genetics for Blondes* (Soho).

OLIVER FENWICK LIGHTING DESIGNER

RSC DEBUT SEASON: *Julius Caesar, The Drunks, The Grain Store.*
theatre includes: *Mary Stuart* (Hipp Theatre, Sweden); *Hedda Gabler* (Gate, Dublin); *Happy Now?* (National Theatre); *Private Lives, The Giant, Glass Eels, Comfort Me With Apples* (Hampstead); *The Lady from the Sea, She Stoops to Conquer* (Birmingham Rep); *The Elephant Man* (Sheffield Lyceum/tour); *Kean* (Apollo, West End); *Solid Gold Cadillac* (Garrick, West End); *The Secret Rapture* (Lyric, West End); *Far from the Madding*

Crowd (ETT); *Jack and the Beanstalk* (Barbican Theatre); *Pure Gold* (Soho); *Henry V, Mirandolina, A Conversation* (Royal Exchange); *Restoration* (Headlong); *My Fair Lady* (Cameron Mackintosh/National Theatre tour); *The Caretaker* (Sheffield Crucible/Tricycle); *The Comedy of Errors, Bird Calls, Iphigenia* (Sheffield Crucible); *Endgame, Noises Off, All My Sons, Doctor Faustus* (Liverpool Playhouse).
opera includes: *Samson et Delilah, Lohengrin, The Trojan Trilogy, The Nose, The Gentle Giant* (Royal Opera House); *The Threepenny Opera* (The Opera Group); *L'Opera Seria* (Batignano Festival).

PASSENGER/ ELDERLY MAN

RSC DEBUT SEASON: Antigonus in *The Winter's Tale*, Cicero/Caesar's Servant/Lepidus/Dardanius in *Julius Caesar*, Passenger/Elderly Man in

The Drunks.
trained: Webber Douglas Academy of Dramatic Art.
theatre includes: In New York, on and off Broadway: *Major Barbara, Playboy of the Western World, Engaged, The Beard of Avon, The Skin Game, Night Over Taos, Life is a Dream, Camille, Two Small Bodies.* Regional theatre includes: *Macbeth, Lion in Winter, Henry V, Blue/Orange, Titus Andronicus, Much Ado about Nothing, Who's Afraid of Virginia Woolf?, Noises Off, The Merchant of Venice.*
film includes: *Larger than Life, Texas Chainsaw Massacre, Save the Dog, A Child's Cry for Help, New York City Serenade, Lucy in the Sky.*

3RD PASSENGER/ 2ND BARFLY

RSC: *The Histories Cycle, Troilus and Cressida, The Mysteries, Everyman.*
this season: Servant in *The Winter's Tale*, Caius Ligarius/Messala in *Julius Caesar*, 3rd Passenger/2nd

Barfly in *The Drunks*.
theatre includes: *Elizabeth* (Kabosh Theatre); *Peri Banez* (Young Vic); *The Story of Yours* (New End); *Of Mice and Men, A View from the Bridge* (Harrogate); *A Streetcar Named Desire* (Royal Lyceum); *The Crucible, Mensch Meier, Blood Wedding, Under Milk Wood* (Haymarket, Leicester); *The Southwark Mysteries* (Globe); *Three Lives of Lucie Cabrol* (Complicite); *Out of a House Walked a Man* (National Theatre); *The Tale of Yvaine* (Royal Festival Hall); *Gormenghast* (David Glass Ensemble); *Crimes of Passion* (Nottingham Playhouse); *Northern Trawl* (Hull Truck).
television includes: *55 Degrees North, Heartbeat, The Long Firm, Emmerdale, Badger, Henry IV Parts 1 and 2, Pie in the Sky, Never the Sinner*.
film includes: *The Gathering, Bridget Jones' Diary, A Dinner of Herbs*.

JAMES HOWARD

2ND SUBORDINATE/ MAN IN HAT
RSC DEBUT SEASON: First Lord in *As You Like It*, 2nd Subordinate/Man in Hat in *The Drunks*.
trained: Bristol Old Vic Theatre School.
theatre includes: *Twelfth Night, Ivanov* (Donmar Warehouse at Wyndham's); *The Revenger's Tragedy* (Southwark Playhouse); *Twelfth Night* (Northcott, Exeter); *Antony and Cleopatra* (Royal Exchange); *The Private Room* (New End); *The Duchess of Malfi, Lear* (National Theatre); *The Merchant of Venice* (Bristol Old Vic).
television includes: *Skins, Emmerdale, Midsomer Murders, The Bill, Natural Wonders, Spooks, Dream Team, The Inspector Lynley Mysteries*.
film includes: *The Oxford Murders, Penelope, Shoot on Sight*.
radio includes: *The Archers, The Last Country House, An Odd Body, Tarnished Wings, Protection, Bloody Stefi, Death of a Village*.

RICHARD KATZ

SERGEY
RSC: *The Winter's Tale, Pericles*.
this season: Touchstone in *As You Like It*, Antipholus of Syracuse in *The Comedy of Errors*, Sergey in *The Drunks*.
theatre includes: *Spyski!* (Lyric Hammersmith/ Peepolykus); *How to Tell the Monsters from the Misfits* (Birmingham Rep); *Señora Carrar's Rifles, Arabian Nights* (Young Vic); *Way to Heaven* (Royal Court); *Faustus* (Northampton); *Measure for Measure* (National Theatre/Complicite); *Life Game* (National Theatre/ Improbable); *Strange Poetry, The Noise of Time, Mnemonic* (Complicite); *The Hanging Man, Angela Carter's Cinderella* (Improbable/Lyric Hammersmith); *The Golden Ass, A Midsummer Night's Dream* (Shakespeare's Globe); *Genoa 01* (Royal Court/Complicite).

television includes: *Thank God You're Here, MI High, The Site, The Passion, Hogfather, The Omid Djalili Show, Green Wing, Hyperdrive, Hustle, Absolute Power, Rome, Nicholas Nickleby.*

film includes: *Measure for Measure, Sixty Six, Start, Enigma, The Last Sin.*

radio includes: *Apes and Angels, The Archers, The Grand Babylon Hotel, Beat the Dog in his Own Kennel.*

TERRY KING
FIGHT DIRECTOR

RSC: Recent productions include: *Othello, Hamlet, A Midsummer Night's Dream, The Histories Cycle, Noughts & Crosses, Antony and Cleopatra, Julius Caesar, King John, Pericles, The Indian Boy, Merry Wives the Musical, A Midsummer Night's Dream, Twelfth Night, As You Like It, Gunpowder Season.*

this season: *As You Like It, The Drunks.*

theatre includes: *The Lord of the Rings, On an Average Day, Ragtime, Chitty Chitty Bang Bang* (West End); *Accidental Death of an Anarchist, Caligula* (Donmar); *King Lear, The Murderers, Fool for Love, Duchess of Malfi, Henry V, Edmund, Jerry Springer the Opera* (National Theatre); *Oleanna, Search and Destroy, Sore Throats* (Royal Court).

opera includes: *Othello* (WNO); *Porgy and Bess* (Glyndebourne); *West Side Story* (York); *Carmen* (ENO).

television includes: *Fell Tiger, A Kind of Innocence, A Fatal Inversion, The Bill, EastEnders, Measure for Measure, Casualty, The Widowing of Mrs. Holroyd, Death of a Salesman.*

HELEN
LEBLIQUE
ASSISTANT
DIRECTOR

RSC DEBUT SEASON: *The Winter's Tale, The Drunks*.

theatre includes: As Director: *Up the Duff* (rehearsed reading); *Trifles, Playgoers, The Twelve Pound Look* (Orange Tree); *A Hitch in Time* (Exeter Northcott, New Writing Festival); *Othello* (Roborough Studio). As Assistant Director: *Far from the Madding Crowd* (English Touring Theatre); *War and Peace* (Shared Experience); *The Madras House, Major Barbara, The Pirates of Penzance, Nan* (Orange Tree); *Hysteria* (Exeter Northcott).

ANNA
MORRISSEY
MOVEMENT
DIRECTOR

RSC: *The Cordelia Dream, The Tragedy of Thomas Hobbes, I'll be the Devil* (RSC/Tricycle), *Timon of Athens* (RSC/Cardboard Citizens).

theatre and opera includes: *Hansel and Gretel* (Opera North); *Hanover Square* (Finborough); *101 Dalmatians* (Theatre Royal, Northampton); *The Barber of Seville, Manon Lescaut* (Opera Holland Park); *Dr Faustus* (Resolution! The Place); *The Tempest, A Warwickshire Testimony, As You Like It, Macbeth* (Bridge House); *The Taming of the Shrew* (Creation Theatre Co.); *Richard III* (Cambridge Arts); *Hamlet* (Cliffords Tower, York); *The Arab-Israeli Cookbook* (Tricycle); *Human Rites* (Southwark Playhouse); *Julius Caesar* (Menier Chocolate Factory); *Tamburlaine the Great* (Rose).

Anna has worked as a practitioner within the RSC Movement Department and taught at E15, Queen Mary and Westfield and Shakespeare's Globe.

ANTHONY NEILSON
DIRECTOR

RSC: *The Big Lie* (Latitude Festival), *God in Ruins* (RSC/Soho).

this season: *The Drunks*.

theatre includes: As a writer and director: *Edward Gant's Amazing Feats of Loneliness* (Theatre Royal, Plymouth); *Stitching* (nominated Evening Standard Most Promising Newcomer. Traverse/ Bush); *Relocated, The Lying Kind* (Royal Court); *The Wonderful World of Dissocia* (Tron/ Edinburgh Lyceum/ Theatre Royal, Plymouth/ Royal Court/national tour); *The Séance* (National Theatre Connections); *The Death of Klinghoffer* (Herald Angel Award. Edinburgh International Festival/Scottish Opera); *The Menu* (National Theatre); *Realism* (Edinburgh International Festival/Lyceum); *Welfare My Lovely* (Traverse); *Normal* (Edinburgh Festival/ Finborough); *Penetrator* (Edinburgh Festival/ Finborourgh/Royal Court); *The Year of the Family* (Finborough); *The Censor* (Writers' Guild Award for Best Fringe Play. Finborough/Royal Court).

film: *The Debt Collector* (writer and director. Winner of the Fipresci International Critics award).

Anthony is currently RSC Literary Associate.

SANDY NEILSON

BABITSKY

RSC: *The Histories Cycle*.

this season: Duke Frederick in *As You Like It*, Babitsky in *The Drunks*.

trained: RSAMD.

theatre includes: *Realism* (National Theatre Studio); *Tales from Hollywood* (Perth Theatre); *Cyprus* (Trafalgar Studios/Mull Theatre); *Macbeth* (Theatre Babel); *Death of a Salesman* (Edinburgh Lyceum); *Ghosts* (Belfast Lyric); *The Duchess of Malfi, The Winter's Tale, A Midsummer Night's Dream, Dancing at Lughnasa* (Dundee Theatre).

television includes: *Mr Hyde, Secret of the Stars, Still Game, Cathedral, Taggart: Penthouse and Pavement, The Greeks, Mr Wymi, The 39 Steps*.

film includes: *Young Adam, A Shot at Glory, The Debt Collector, The Winter Guest*.

JONJO O'NEILL

ILYA

RSC: *Head/Case, Believe What You Will, A New Way to Please You, Sejanus: His Fall, Speaking Like Magpies*.

this season: Orlando in *As You Like It*, Dromio of Syracuse in *The Comedy of Errors*, Ilya in *The Drunks*.

theatre includes: *King Lear* (Liverpool Everyman/Young Vic); *Someone Else's Shoes* (Soho); *Faustus* (Hampstead); *Paradise Lost* (Northampton Theatre Royal); *A View from the Bridge, The David Hare Trilogy* (Birmingham Rep); *Observe the Sons of Ulster* (Pleasance); *Dolly West's Kitchen* (Haymarket, Leicester); *Half a Sixpence* (West Yorkshire Playhouse); *Translations* (Watford Palace/ tour); *Dick Whittington* (Sadler's Wells); *Of Thee I Sing* (Bridewell Theatre); *The Frogs* (Nottingham Playhouse/ tour); *Refuge* (Royal Court).

television includes: *The History of Mr Polly, I Do, The Year London Blew Up, I Fought the Law, Bay College, Murphy's Law: Manic Monday, A Touch of Frost, Charlie's*

Angel, Band of Brothers, Holby City, Thin Ice, Extremely Dangerous, Sunburn, Risk. **film includes:** Defiance, Fakers.

PETER PEVERLEY

YOUNG KOSTYA/ 1ST BARFLY
RSC DEBUT SEASON: Jaques De Boys/Dennis in As You Like It, Balthazar in The Comedy of Errors, Young Kostya/1st Barfly in The Drunks.
trained: Newcastle College.
theatre includes: Romeo and Juliet, Twelfth Night, Threepenny Opera, Great Expectations, Animal Farm, Clockwork Orange, Grimm's Tales, The Ballroom of Romance, Elmer McCurdy Rides Again, Pinocchio, Edmund, The Dumb Waiter, Glengarry Glen Ross, The Long Line, Andorra, The Snow Queen, Son of Man (Northern Stage Ensemble 1998-2006); The Firework-Maker's Daughter (Told by an Idiot/Sheffield Crucible); The Venetian Twins (Octagon, Bolton); Greenfingers (Live Theatre/Northern Stage);

Cabaret, Oh! What a Lovely War (Live Theatre, Newcastle); Beautiful Game (Theatre Royal, Newcastle); Get Off at Gateshead (Gala, Durham); Accounts (Northumberland Theatre Co.); Much Ado about Nothing (Mad Alice Theatre Co.); The Little Waster (one man show).
television includes: Byker Grove, Emmerdale, Harry, Spender, The Parables.
writing: The Little Waster.
composition includes: The Golden Bird, Black Eyed Roses (Northern Stage).

TOM PIPER
DESIGNER
RSC designs include: The Histories Cycle, Macbeth, The Broken Heart, Spring Awakening, A Patriot for Me, Much Ado about Nothing, The Spanish Tragedy, Bartholomew Fair, Measure for Measure, Troilus and Cressida, A Month in the Country, A Midsummer Night's Dream, Romeo and Juliet, Henry VI, Richard III, The Tempest, King Lear, Twelfth Night, Hamlet.
this season: As You Like It, The Drunks, The Grain Store, Antony and Cleopatra.
theatre designs include: The Birthday Party, Blinded by the Sun, Oh! What a Lovely War (National Theatre); Miss Julie (Haymarket); Frame 312, A Lie of the Mind, Three Days of Rain, Helpless (Donmar); Pants, Mince?, Duchess of

Malfi, Twelfth Night, Happy Days (Dundee Rep); Denial, Les Liaisons Dangereuses, Ghosts (Bristol Old Vic); The Danny Crowe Show (Bush); The Frogs, The Cherry Orchard (Nottingham Playhouse); Stiff!, The Master Builder (Lyceum, Edinburgh); The Crucible, Six Characters in Search of an Author (Abbey, Dublin); Backpay, Cockroach, Who? (Royal Court); Zorro (Garrick); Spyski! (Lyric Hammersmith); Dealer's Choice (Menier Chocolate Factory/Trafalgar); Fall (Traverse).

NICK POWELL
MUSIC AND
SOUND DESIGNER
RSC: The Big Lie (Latitude Festival), God in Ruins (RSC/Soho).
this season: The Drunks, The Grain Store.
theatre includes: As composer and sound designer: Panic (Improbable); The Vertical Hour, Relocated (Royal Court); Bonheur (Composer. Comedie Francais, Paris). Music and songs for: Urtain, Marat/ Sade (Spanish National Theatre/Animalario); Realism (Edinburgh International Festival); The Wonderful World of Dissocia (Winner of Best Production for TMA and Scottish Theatre awards); Pyrenees (TMA Best New Play), Mercury Fur, The Drowned World, Tiny Dynamite (co-produced

with Frantic Assembly), *Splendour* (Paines Plough). Co-creator and composer: *The Wolves in the Walls* (National Theatre of Scotland/ Improbable).

As Musical Director of Glasgow's Suspect Culture Nick developed and scored twelve shows including *Timeless, Mainstream, Casanova, Lament, One, Two…, 800m* and *Futurology: A Global Review* as well as numerous workshops and performances throughout the world.

film and television includes: *Beneath the Veil* (BAFTA winner), *Luther, Death in Gaza* (BAFTA winner).

music includes: He is one half of Oskar, who have just released *LP:2*, the follow-up to their debut album *Air Conditioning*.

NINA RAINE
TRANSLATOR

RSC DEBUT SEASON: *The Drunks*.

trained: Oxford University.

theatre includes: Nina began her career as a trainee director at the Royal Court Theatre. She dramaturged and directed the hard-hitting verbatim play *Unprotected* at the Liverpool Everyman, for which she won both the TMA Best Director award and the Amnesty International Freedom of Expression award for an Outstanding Production on a Human Rights Theme. Her debut play, *Rabbit*, was shortlisted for the Verity Bargate award 2004.

It premiered at the Old Red Lion Theatre in 2006 and after a sell-out run transferred to the Trafalgar Studios in the West End. She has just completed her second play, *Tiger Country*, and is now under commission to the Royal Court Theatre.

SOPHIE **RUSSELL**

PLUMP WOMAN/ WOMAN IN BERET

RSC DEBUT SEASON: Audrey in *As You Like It*, Abbess in *The Comedy of Errors*, Plump Woman/ Woman in Beret in *The Drunks*.

trained: Middlesex University, Ecole Nationale Superieure des Arts et Techniques du Theatre, Paris.

theatre includes: *The Good Soul of Szechuan* (Young Vic); *Spyski!* (Peepolykus/Lyric Hammersmith); *The Crock of Gold, Metamorphosis, Alice Through the Looking Glass, The Tinderbox* (London Bubble); *The Chaingang Gang, Meat and Two Veg, The Ratcatcher of Hamelin* (Cartoon de Salvo/Battersea Arts Centre); *Invisible Town* (National Theatre Studio); *The Bitches' Ball* (Assembly

Rooms, Edinburgh); *Great Expectations* (Shifting Sands Theatre Co.); *Oliver Twist* (International tour); *I am Dandy* (David Gale Ensemble); *Cinderella* (Palace, Westcliff); *A Christmas Carol* (Palace, Newark).

television: *Wire in the Blood*.

CLARENCE **SMITH**

3RD BABITSKY/ 1ST POLICEMAN

RSC: *Noughts & Crosses, The Winter's Tale, Pericles, King Lear, Don Juan*.

this season: Duke Ferdinand in *As You Like It*, 3rd Babitsky/1st Policeman in *The Drunks*.

theatre includes: *King Lear* (Headlong); *Pure Gold, Shrieks of Laughter* (Soho); *Design for Living, Les Blancs* (Royal Exchange); *Macbeth* (Arcola); *The Storm* (Almeida); *As You Like It* (Tokyo Globe); *The Honest Whore, The Merchant of Venice* (Shakespeare's Globe); *King Lear, Chasing the Moment* (Southwark Playhouse); *Romeo and Juliet, Fuente Ovejuna, Yerma, Blood Brothers, Hiawatha* (Bristol Old Vic); *The Jamaican Airman Foresees his Death, Our

Country's Good, Charity Event (Royal Court).

television includes: *Doctors, The Last Detective, Holby City, The Eustace Bros, Waking the Dead, EastEnders, Undercover Cops, Daylight Robbery, The Bill, Sharman.*

film includes: *Mexican Standoff, Star Wars, The Dinner, What my Mother Told Me.*

other work includes: *The Remnant, Johnny was a Good Man* (writer/director), *Ragamuffin, Some Kind of Hero* (director/co-producer) (Double Edge).

2ND PASSENGER/ EFREMOV

RSC DEBUT SEASON: Sir Oliver Martext in *As You Like It*, Solinus in *The Comedy of Errors*, 2nd Passenger/ Efremov in *The Drunks*.

trained: Rose Bruford College.

theatre includes: *The Venetian Twins* (Bolton Octagon); *Rapunzel* (Kneehigh at Queen Elizabeth Hall/ Broadway); *The Car Cemetery* (Gate); *Martin Guerre, The Thieves Carnival* (Watermill); *The Soldier's Fortune*

(Young Vic); *Tristan and Yseult* (Kneehigh at Sydney/Wellington Festival); *Twelfth Night, The Hired Man* (Theatre by the Lake); *Caledonian Road* (Almeida); *Junk* (Bristol Old Vic); *Johnny Blue* (Oxford Stage Co.); *Gulliver* (Riverside Studios); *Nicholas Nickleby* (Red Shift); *Holes* (Stratford East).

television includes: *Clone, Supergrass, Go Now, The Bill, Dream Team, Jenner, Jump.*

film includes: *The Mummy, Over Exposed, The Sobering.*

NATASHA YOUNG

RSC: *The Merry Wives of Windsor, Coriolanus* (RSC/ Old Vic), *The Lion, the Witch and the Wardrobe* (Sadler's Wells).

this season: Emilia in *The Winter's Tale*, Portia in *Julius Caesar*, Natasha in *The Drunks*.

trained: University of Exeter.

theatre includes: *Corporate Rock* (Nabokov); *The Lady from the Sea* (Birmingham Rep); *Songs of Grace and Redemption* (Theatre503); *The French Lieutenant's Woman* (Yvonne Arnaud/ No. 1 tour); *As You Desire* (Playhouse, London); *Time*

and the Conways (Theatre Royal Bath/No.1 tour); *First Love, Kishon Brook* (International Playwrighting Festival, Royal Court); *A Chaste Maid in Cheapside* (Almeida/No.1 tour); *Les Liaisons Dangereuses* (Liverpool Playhouse); *A Midsummer Night's Dream* (Albery); *The Importance of Being Earnest* (Deptford Albany); *Queer Dorset Bastard* (Camden Etcetera); *The Stringless Maisonette* (Orange Tree); *The Swell* (Theatre Alibi).

television includes: *Britain's Nazi King, Doctors, The Robinsons, Waking the Dead, Offenders, Newsnight.*

film: *Alan's Breakfast.*

radio: *Levitt in London.*

Production Acknowledgments

Scenery, set painting, properties, costumes, armoury, wigs and make-up by RSC Workshops, Stratford-upon-Avon. Joe Hull of High Performance Rigging with Steve Robinson and Alex Poulter. Production photographer Ellie Kurttz. Access performances provided by Janet Jackson and Ridanne Sheridan.

TRANSFORMING OUR
THEATRES

In 1932, following the 1926 fire which destroyed much of the original Shakespeare Memorial Theatre, a new proscenium arch space opened in Stratford-upon-Avon, designed by Elizabeth Scott. Now known as the Royal Shakespeare Theatre the building boasted a spacious, fan-shaped auditorium housed inside Scott's art-deco inspired designs.

And now the RST is undergoing another transformation from a proscenium stage to a one-room space allowing the epic and intimate to play side by side.

At the heart of the project will be a new auditorium. Seating around 1,000 people, the stage thrusts into the audience with theatregoers seated on three sides, bringing the actor and audience closer together for a more intimate theatre experience.

The new space will transform the existing theatre, retaining the key Art Deco elements of the building. A new Theatre Tower with viewing platform, theatre square for outdoor performances, a linking foyer to join the Royal Shakespeare and Swan Theatres together for the first time, and new public spaces are central to the new building.

7,000 people have already supported the transformation from over 40 countries worldwide. To find out more and to play your part visit **www.rsc.org.uk/appeal**

Advantage
West Midlands

The regional leader for
developing economic prosperity

Supported by

The National Lottery®

through Arts Council England

ARTS COUNCIL
ENGLAND

SUPPORT THE RSC

As a registered charity the Royal Shakespeare Company relies on public support and generosity.

There are many ways you can help the RSC including joining Shakespeare's Circle, RSC Patrons, through Corporate support or by leaving a bequest.

RSC Patrons and Shakespeare's Circle

By supporting the RSC through Shakespeare's Circle and RSC Patrons you can help us to create outstanding theatre and give as many people as possible a richer and fuller understanding of Shakespeare and theatre practice. In return you receive benefits including priority booking and invitations to exclusive supporters' events. Shakespeare's Circle Membership starts at £8.50 per month.

Help Secure our Future

Legacy gifts ensure that the RSC can develop and flourish in the years to come, bringing the pleasure of theatre to future generations that you yourself have enjoyed.

Corporate Partnerships

The RSC has a national and internationally recognised brand, whilst retaining its unique positioning as a Warwickshire-based organisation. It tours more than any other UK-based arts organisation and has annual residencies in London and Newcastle upon Tyne. As such it is uniquely placed to offer corporate partnership benefits across the globe.

The Company's experienced Corporate Development team can create bespoke packages around their extensive range of classical and new work productions, education programmes and online activity. These are designed to fulfil business objectives such as building client relationships, encouraging staff retention and accessing specific segments of the RSC's audience. A prestigious programme of corporate hospitality and membership packages are also available.

For more information, please telephone **01789 403470**.

For detailed information about opportunities to support the work of the RSC, visit **www.rsc.org.uk/support**

GET MORE INVOLVED

RSC Membership

Become an RSC Member and enjoy a wide range of benefits.

Full Member £36 (per year).
As an RSC Full Member you receive up to four weeks' priority booking with a dedicated hotline into the RSC Box Office, Director's selection of four exclusive production photographs per year, regular Members' newsletters, access to Members' only web pages, special ticket offers – save £20 on two top price tickets in Stratford (conditions apply) and 10% discount in RSC Shops, Mail Order, RSC Short Breaks and at The Courtyard Theatre Café Bar.

Associate Member £15 (per year).
As an RSC Associate Member you receive priority booking of up to two weeks with a dedicated hotline into the RSC Box Office, regular Members' newsletters and 10% discount in The Courtyard Theatre Café Bar and with RSC Short Breaks.

Gift Membership.
All membership levels can be bought as a gift.

Overseas Membership.
This is available for those living outside the UK.

To find out more or to join, please contact the Membership Office on **01789 403440** (Monday-Friday 9am-5pm) or visit **www.rsc.org.uk/membership**

GET MORE INVOLVED

RSC Friends

As a network of the RSC's most active supporters, RSC Friends are important advocates for the Company, encouraging people to enjoy a closer relationship with the RSC and its work on and off stage.

Joining the Friends costs £20 a year and is open to RSC Full and Associate Members. Benefits include a lively programme of events plus a quarterly Friends' Newsletter and further opportunities to become more closely involved with the RSC.

For more information or to join, please contact the Membership Office on **01789 403440** or join online at **www.rsc.org.uk/membership**

RSC Online

www.rsc.org.uk

Visit the RSC website to Select Your Own Seat and book tickets online, keep up to date with the latest news, sign up for regular email updates or simply learn more about Shakespeare in our Exploring Shakespeare section.

THE DRUNKS

Mikhail and Vyacheslav Durnenkov

Translated by Nina Raine

From a literal translation by Maria Kozlovskaya

2

Characters

A FOOL
BABITSKY
ILYA
PASSENGER
SECOND PASSENGER
THIRD PASSENGER
CONDUCTOR
POLICEMAN
RAILWAY WORKER
MAYOR
MAYOR'S AIDE (KOSTYA)
MAN IN HAT
KOTOMTSEV
ELDERLY POLICEMAN
EFREMOV
NATASHA
IVAN
SERGEY
VASSILIEV
SAVELIEV

FIRST BARFLY
SECOND BARFLY
PLUMP WOMAN
SECOND BABITSKY
THIRD BABITSKY
PRETTY GIRL
STAFF PHOTOGRAPHER
WOMAN IN BERET
ELDERLY MAN
FIRST ILYA
SECOND ILYA
THIRD ILYA

Plus various other subordinates, policemen, guards, children, townspeople and a band.

This text went to press before the end of rehearsals and so may differ slightly from the play as performed.

Prologue

As the audience comes in, the ACTORS *file onto the stage. Each receives a small shot glass full of vodka. They stare longingly at the drinks they cannot drink yet.*

Eventually, clearance is given and another actor – dressed as a traditional FOOL *– joins them onstage. They animate with excitement when they see him.*

He is presented with his own drink and then he shouts at the audience:

FOOL. Ladies and gentlemen – we are proud to present...

And, shouting as if it were a toast:

ACTORS. *The Drunks!*

...they swig back their drinks.

FOOL (*shouting*). Scene One!!

He will announce all the scenes this way.

Music begins and suddenly all is action: the ACTORS *take their places, seated around the stage.* BABITSKY *is helped up onto the catwalk and walks forward. The music stops suddenly, and then...*

Scene One

BABITSKY *addresses the* CHILDREN.

BABITSKY. Well – I'm glad that we've met. Not that you had much choice in the matter. You were always going to end up with me; like your mothers and fathers before you.

He singles out ILYA.

Ilya, isn't it? I remember your father. Let's hope you inherited his better traits. I noticed you can wiggle your ears, just like he could. There are more useful skills to have in life, but still – for now, that's the only distinctive thing about you.

He addresses all the CHILDREN.

But I'm going to help you all; to become someone. Someone special. Unique, if you like. There's only one thing you have to do.

Believe in me.

You don't need to love me, like you love your parents. You just need to believe in me. Even when I tell you things that seem unbelievable, you just have to remember: the only truths in this world are the ones I'll tell you.

He singles out another child, KOSTYA.

So – what do you think? Kostya, isn't it?

KOSTYA *nods.*

Good boy. Do you believe in me, Kostya?

KOSTYA *nods.*

(*Suddenly harsh.*) Well, you shouldn't!

KOSTYA *shrinks in fear.*

I asked you to believe me, and you immediately agreed! But we've only just met. What proof do you have that I know what I'm talking about? What have I ever done for you? Nothing. I could be just some old man, wandered in off the street. So why should you believe in me?

KOSTYA *doesn't know, and is a little scared.* BABITSKY *softens.*

Well, I'll tell you why.

BABITSKY *shows some official document, or perhaps dons an item of clothing.*

Because I'm your teacher. That's why. That's the proof.

(*Precisely.*) I. Am. Your. Teacher.

He lets this sink in.

Now – go and think about that. Tomorrow, you start a new life.

They don't move.

On you go.

All the CHILDREN *run out, except for* ILYA, KOSTYA, NATASHA *and* SERGEY.

BABITSKY *is leaving, but he turns and addresses* ILYA.

Ilya!

ILYA *bolts to attention.*

I can wiggle my ears as well.

BABITSKY *lowers his head and wiggles his ears.*

Scene Two

Various PASSENGERS *attempt to make their way along a moving train, holding full-to-the-brim shot glasses of vodka.* ILYA *is being followed by a* PASSENGER.

PASSENGER. Do I know you from somewhere? We met, or something?

ILYA. I don't think so, sorry...

PASSENGER. No. I get it. You just got one of those faces. You know, bog-standard. You look like quite a few people I know. Don't get me wrong – good people, reliable people. 'Stolid.' Do I mean stolid?... Drink?

They arrive at a cabin, where they sit. ILYA *is tempted, but...*

ILYA. I'd better not.

The PASSENGER *pours a glass.*

PASSENGER. Suit yourself. (*He toasts.*) To them that makes the world go round.

He drinks.

So... why're you not drinking then? Scared you won't be able to stop? Hope it's not principles, standards. Between you and me, I don't trust a teetotaller. You don't know where you stand with them. Like politicians: most of them don't drink – enough said. I mean, *I* was a teetotaller, believe it or not, until I was twenty. But when I had my first drink – start of a new life. More relaxed, better at socialising, started to mingle – all that... bollocks. Don't remember the exact details, but quality of life – no comparison! I'd wake up in the morning – clueless, still shitfaced. Sit there, trying to remember what happened the night before... no fucking idea. All that was left of my memory was a sort of... faded fax. Genius, the memory loss you get with boozing. Past – erased! It's a fucking brilliant invention, drink. The internal-combustion engine, the wheel, the radio, and now – this. Don't get me wrong, I'm not forcing you, but...

The PASSENGER *passes* ILYA *the glass.* ILYA *hesitantly takes it in his hands.*

ILYA. The doctors said I shouldn't.

PASSENGER. Fucking doctors! This is medicine, mate. Medicine you take in very large doses. Down it. Go on. You'll feel better straightaway.

ILYA *looks at the glass dubiously.*

ILYA. I haven't had a drink in a long time.

PASSENGER. Oh, I get you. You've had some time off. And there you are. Standing at the edge of the sea. Bit nervous. You inch in up to the knees. To the thighs. Dreading the moment it nips your nutsack. But all that's just dragging out the torture. You've got to just dive right in! And then – !

ILYA *brings the glass close to his mouth but doesn't drink.*

Come on, get it down you! You know what? You're bloody lucky. I bloody envy you, mate. It'll be like the first taste again... the first sip... the first anything...

The glass almost touches ILYA*'s lips but he hesitates.*

Oh, I see. You want your privacy. It's a private moment, I understand. I shall avert my gaze.

The PASSENGER *turns away.* ILYA *cautiously drinks from the glass. The alcohol is gone, but* ILYA*'s Adam's apple still moves, as he drinks the smell of the alcohol, the shape of the glass, drinks the world and the darkness he is now submerged in. A* SECOND PASSENGER *appears on* ILYA*'s right, then a* THIRD.

There you are. Isn't that better? Back to normal.

SECOND PASSENGER. Back to the real world.

PASSENGER. Back to reality.

THIRD PASSENGER. Back home.

ILYA....What's it like there?

PASSENGER. There? It's cold there now, very cold.

SECOND PASSENGER. It's brass fucking monkeys.

PASSENGER. The streets're icy –

THIRD PASSENGER. People falling over –

SECOND PASSENGER. Breaking their legs –

PASSENGER. Breaking their hips.

THIRD PASSENGER. And everyone's breath steaming on the air.

PASSENGER. It's impossible to get warm. One old guy froze to death while he was taking a piss.

SECOND PASSENGER. There he was, just stood there –

PASSENGER. With an arc of frozen piss between his dick and the ground.

THIRD PASSENGER. God is more forgiving of them that dies in winter.

ILYA *puts his glass back down.*

SECOND PASSENGER. The kids made a snowwoman in the schoolyard. Tits, arse, pubes made out of twigs...

THIRD PASSENGER. You should have seen its expression...

PASSENGER. Like Putin with knockers.

The THIRD PASSENGER *imitates the snowwoman's expression. The* PASSENGERS *all laugh. Steam comes out of their mouths.*

THIRD PASSENGER. Everything that can freeze has frozen.

SECOND PASSENGER. Even the smells.

THIRD PASSENGER. Dogs can't smell their owners apart.

SECOND PASSENGER. People only wash once a week, they're not even sweating any more.

PASSENGER. It is very cold there.

THIRD PASSENGER. It's too cold even to fuck. There won't be many children born next autumn.

SECOND PASSENGER. But they'll be healthy little buggers.

ILYA (*suddenly*). I was born in the winter.

THIRD PASSENGER. Like your son!

ILYA. Like my son!

PASSENGER. Now there's a good boy.

SECOND PASSENGER. He's a good boy. He loves dancing.

PASSENGER. Oh, he loves dancing.

THIRD PASSENGER. Mummy claps her hands, and he dances.

SECOND PASSENGER. She says he's taking lessons.

PASSENGER. Clear he's got talent.

THIRD PASSENGER. Fantastic sense of rhythm.

SECOND PASSENGER. Lovely lad.

PASSENGER. Got a sister now.

THIRD PASSENGER. Born this winter.

SECOND PASSENGER. Now *that* is a child with no sense of rhythm whatsoever.

PASSENGER. They do love their kids there.

THIRD PASSENGER. They love their kids to bits.

PASSENGER. They spoil them bloody rotten.

THIRD PASSENGER. Love instead of a proper upbringing.

PASSENGER. Love instead of a lot of things there.

The PASSENGERS *laugh, and steam comes out of their mouths.* ILYA *looks at them uncomprehendingly.*

ILYA. How does he dance?

SECOND PASSENGER. Who?

THIRD PASSENGER. Your son?

PASSENGER. What's it to you? He dances, that's what he does. He's dancing, you're sitting with us, and everyone's doing their thing. Jesus!

ILYA *stands up too, and staggers.*

ILYA. I want to dance too... I've got rhythm.

The PASSENGERS *start clapping their hands rhythmically.* ILYA *throws his arms open and springs from one leg to the other, like a bear. Pause.* ILYA *sits down. The* PASSENGERS *are silent.*

What else does he like doing?

PASSENGER (*irritably*). Can't you just leave it?

ILYA. I haven't been there for a long time... I want to know...

SECOND PASSENGER. Why? Relax! No one's worrying about you.

THIRD PASSENGER. Everyone's doing fine without you.

ILYA (*surprised*). What do you mean, 'everyone's doing fine'?

PASSENGER. Oh, you know. Out of sight, out of mind. They've forgotten about you.

ILYA *staggers, stands up and grabs the* PASSENGER *violently by the collar, dragging him towards himself.*

ILYA. What do you mean, 'forgotten'? What are you talking about, cunt? I'm going home, d'you hear me? Home!!

The SECOND PASSENGER *and* THIRD PASSENGER *suddenly disappear. The remaining* PASSENGER, *his eyes bulging with fear, stares at* ILYA.

PASSENGER. The fuck are you doing, you psycho? Get off me!

ILYA. I'll fucking tear you apart! I'll rip your eyes out!

ILYA *bends over the terrified* PASSENGER.

PASSENGER. Help!

The door of the compartment opens: a CONDUCTOR *and* POLICEMEN *grab hold of* ILYA. *They twist his arms behind his back. The* PASSENGER *cowers in a corner.*

CONDUCTOR. All right, nice and calm, now –

PASSENGER. Get me a seat away from him! He's a fucking nut, I've been assaulted! I want an upgrade!

POLICEMAN. How much did you drink?

PASSENGER. Only a shot and then he started on me! You're not right in the fucking head, mate!

POLICEMAN (*to* ILYA). Can I see your papers, please?

PASSENGER. He's a fucking psycho!

Scene Three

The train station. On the platform, shifting from foot to foot to keep warm, stand the MAYOR *and his* AIDE. *The* MAYOR *is clutching a photograph of* ILYA. *Further away, their collars up, stand the rest of his* ENTOURAGE *and a small brass* BAND. *A short* RAILWAY WORKER *in a railway-staff cap runs up to the* MAYOR.

RAILWAY WORKER. Boris Ivanovich, I can't find him.

MAYOR. What do you mean, 'can't find him'?

RAILWAY WORKER. It's like he's evaporated or something. I just don't get it. He should have been on this train –

MAYOR. You fucking idiot. I'll have you hanged.

RAILWAY WORKER. Hanged? That's a bit much! He was on the list of passengers. But now, dunno why, he's not on the train.

MAYOR. Have you shown his picture to the station staff? Someone must have seen him.

RAILWAY WORKER. Maybe he's been – like – horribly
   mutilated?

MAYOR. I'll hang every bastard one of you.

RAILWAY WORKER. I don't think there's enough posts –

MAYOR. You're fired. Kostya, fire this fucker.

AIDE. I'm afraid you're fired.

   The RAILWAY WORKER *walks away, dejected.*

   Definitely been a miscommunication. Maybe he got off a
   stop early? He does have shell shock, after all.

MAYOR. How bad is he?

AIDE. Bad. Apparently they had to piece his skull back together bit by bit.

MAYOR. Terrible…

AIDE. Yes, he nearly died…

MAYOR. No, this is bloody terrible. This cock-up. It would
   have made such a beautiful story: 'The Mayor and the In-
   valid.' When my dad came back from the war, there were
   flowers, the whole train was covered with flowers, the works.
   I thought we could put on the same sort of show. It's what
   you're taught in school, isn't it: 'A Hero's Welcome.' You've
   got to have a brass band playing, women weeping, lots of
   dancing –

   A funny MAN *in a furry hat with ear-flaps runs up.*

MAN IN HAT. Boris Ivanovich, should I let the band go?

MAYOR. No. Let the fuckers play. We're paying them, aren't we?

MAN IN HAT. No…

MAYOR. And something cheerful, for God's sake. (*To his*
   AIDE.) Christ. Kostya – let's get out of here.

   The MAYOR *and* AIDE *leave. The* MAN IN THE HAT *runs
   over to the* BAND *and waves his hand. The* BAND *starts to
   play.*

Scene Four

The police station. KOTOMTSEV*'s office.* KOTOMTSEV *is at his desk.* ILYA *sits on a chair.* KOTOMTSEV *looks at* ILYA*'s passport. He puts the passport aside. He looks at* ILYA.

KOTOMTSEV. So. What have you got to say for yourself?

ILYA. I don't know. What am I supposed to say?

KOTOMTSEV (*looking at him narrowly*). You taking the piss?

ILYA. No, I've never done this before.

KOTOMTSEV. Never done what before? Got pissed? Or gone mental on a train?

ILYA. No. I have. I mean, got drunk. Before. But then they told me I shouldn't drink. I didn't think –

KOTOMTSEV. What fucker told you not to drink?

KOTOMTSEV *meanwhile has picked up* ILYA*'s military certificate, and is turning the pages. He puts it next to* ILYA*'s passport.*

ILYA. The hospital. The doctors. After the shell shock. I've been in hospital for three –

KOTOMTSEV (*looking back at the passport, interrupting*). Very familiar surname. What school did you go to?

ILYA. The one near the bridge.

KOTOMTSEV. Oh, I was at the stone one!

ILYA. My dad went there!

KOTOMTSEV. Your dad? Not called Tolik, was he?

ILYA. Yes!

KOTOMTSEV (*fiercely*). He was a cunt!

KOTOMTSEV *abruptly flicks* ILYA *hard on the forehead – indicating that* ILYA *has lost a bet.* ILYA *shakes his head, bemused.*

Your dad lost a bet with me. We had an argument – who was going to make their mark first in the world. I won. Obviously. Course, I can't tell *him* that now. Cos he's fucking dead. So I'm transmitting the message through you.

Pause.

So. What's the plan, Stan?

ILYA.…'Stan'?

KOTOMTSEV. We had a teacher at our school, a dessicated old fuck he was. But he always said, 'You don't work, you don't exist. If you want to exist, you have to work.' He also said minus times plus is minus, and minus times minus is plus, he was a CUNT!!

Before ILYA *can say anything, an* ELDERLY POLICEMAN *comes in with a large parcel.*

ELDERLY POLICEMAN. Here you go, Viktor Viktorovich. From the workshop. They said to say the other stuff'll be ready soon.

KOTOMTSEV *eagerly unwraps the bundle and pulls out what looks like an antique Restoration sword.*

KOTOMTSEV. Delilah! Daddy's missed you.

KOTOMTSEV *rolls up one of his sleeves, grabs the sword and stretches it out admiringly.*

(*Indicating his arm.*) Feel that. Like iron. And I can hold it like that for half an hour straight. Check out the veins!

KOTOMTSEV *suddenly lashes out, swiping the air above* ILYA*'s head.* ILYA *cowers, covering his head with his hands, ineffectually, like a child.*

Scare the shit out of you, did I? Wait till you see me in chain mail.

KOTOMTSEV *kisses the blade and puts it on the table. He looks at it, deep in thought.*

(*Quietly.*) It's okay. We can do it. (*To* ILYA.) What are you looking at, cripple?

ILYA. I am not a cripple.

KOTOMTSEV. If you can't drink, you're a cripple. I'm bored now. Fuck off. And if I see you again you'll end up in the river with this up your arse.

He flourishes the sword.

Efremov! See him out.

EFREMOV *hustles* ILYA *out.*

Scene Five

NATASHA*'s flat.* NATASHA *sits in a downy shawl at the table, watching television. There is a knock on the door. She gets up and shuffles over to it in her slippers.*

NATASHA. Who is it?

ILYA. It's me.

NATASHA. Who's 'me'?

ILYA. Ilya.

NATASHA *freezes on the spot. Then she cautiously opens the door, and takes a couple of steps back.* ILYA *walks into the flat. He's holding various coloured plastic bags.*

Pause.

Is it okay? That I just dropped by?

Pause.

I won't stay long.

NATASHA. It's fine. Come in.

ILYA *awkwardly tries to unlace his boot.*

Don't worry about that. Sit down.

ILYA *sits down at the table.* NATASHA *sits opposite him.*

ILYA. So. How are you?

NATASHA. Good, thanks. You?

ILYA. Yeah, I'm good.

Pause.

NATASHA. I don't really know what to say.

ILYA. No, me neither.

Pause.

NATASHA. I'm sorry I didn't come to see you. In the hospital.

Pause. ILYA *nods.*

ILYA. It's okay.

Pause. Suddenly, a boy of six or seven, IVAN, *comes into the room.* ILYA *stands. An awkward silence.*

NATASHA. Ivan, where are your manners? Say hello.

IVAN. Hello.

ILYA *looks at the boy with great attention. The boy becomes awkward and he looks at his mother, confused.*

NATASHA. This man… This man knew you when you were very small.

Pause. ILYA *realises that he needs to say something.*

ILYA. How's school? You working hard?

Pause. NATASHA *breathes in deeply.*

NATASHA. He's learning to dance.

ILYA. I know. Folk dancing.

NATASHA. Go on. Show him how you dance.

IVAN *looks sceptically at his mother. He's not planning to dance, least of all in front of a stranger.*

IVAN. My friends are waiting for me –

NATASHA. Show us your dance first. And then you can go. We'll clap for you.

IVAN unwillingly puts his skates on the floor. NATASHA turns to ILYA, animatedly. She shows him how he needs to clap.

Like this. To give him the rhythm.

NATASHA claps, slowly but rhythmically. IVAN, throwing his arms wide, dances. He finishes and bows. NATASHA applauds loudly.

(*Proudly.*) His teacher says he's the best in his class. He says he dances with his whole spirit.

IVAN. Can I go now?

NATASHA nods and the boy leaves. Silence falls again.

NATASHA. Thank you. For not saying anything. He's too young to understand.

Pause.

It's for the best.

ILYA. I suppose so.

NATASHA. And Nikolai takes good care of him; he spoils him, really.

NATASHA stands up and begins to walk around the room, nervously. ILYA stands up. He picks up his bag. NATASHA turns to him unexpectedly.

I don't understand you, Ilya.

ILYA. What?

NATASHA. Don't you *give* a fuck? About anything?

Don't you want to shout at me… or call me a bitch… Don't you want to slap me in the face?

ILYA. Should I?

NATASHA. Yes. You should.

ILYA *awkwardly goes over to* NATASHA *and hits her weakly on the cheek.*

Harder.

ILYA *looks at her. He walks away.*

(*She shouts after him.*) Harder!

Scene Six

ILYA *walks down the street. He pulls a pack of cigarettes out of his pocket.* SERGEY *comes up to him.*

SERGEY. Ilya?

ILYA *starts, and drops his cigarette.*

Hello, stranger!

ILYA. ...He didn't know who I was.

SERGEY. Who?

ILYA. My son.

SERGEY (*wiping the smile from his face*). Oh. I see. Well – what can you do? He's only a kid. (*He smiles again.*) But I knew who you were! Didn't I?

Pause.

ILYA. Yes. Sergey.

SERGEY. Give us a hug.

They hug.

I didn't think I'd ever see you again!

ILYA. I got... My head...

SERGEY *halts him with a gesture.*

SERGEY. I know, I know. I know all about it. You don't have to tell me. Better that way. Listen. They just opened a new vodka bar round the corner.

ILYA. I can't drink. (*He points to his head.*)

SERGEY. Fair enough. We can have a chat.

ILYA. All right.

> ILYA *and* SERGEY *pick up the bag, one strap each, and leave.*

Scene Seven

The banya. It has seven shelves. On the top sits KOTOMTSEV, *and three shelves lower down, his five* SUBORDINATES. *The* SUBORDINATES *all have towels wrapped around their waists.*

KOTOMTSEV. Yesterday, right. I was shagging this big-arsed cadet. For an hour and forty minutes. How about that? Oi! Vassiliev! How long can you fuck a bird?

> VASSILIEV, *a short, balding man, stands up. He looks around him helplessly.*

And no fibbing. You're a shit liar.

VASSILIEV (*wincing*). On average? About ten minutes.

KOTOMTSEV. Like a fucking sewing machine!

> *Everyone laughs.*

Saveliev? What about you?

> SAVELIEV *gets up, automatically making a movement as if to adjust his non-existent tie.*

SAVELIEV. Twenty-three minutes, seventeen seconds, precisely. When the wife and I decided to conceive Mashka, we noted down the times. That was the average.

KOTOMTSEV. Good lad! So, like I say. I come into this bird's bedroom – completely starkers except for my samurai *katana* – she was that shocked, she almost shat the sheets! And I just circled her, like a – like this – pantherlike – then – I pounced. She was gagging for it. Shaking all over. Seriously – I gave her the fuck of her life.

At this point, the MAYOR *comes into the banya, with his* ENTOURAGE *of five. The* MAYOR *climbs up onto the top shelf, and* KOTOMTSEV, *very unwillingly, goes down a level. The* MAYOR'S SUBORDINATES *and* KOTOMTSEV'S *get muddled up and it's hard to tell the two groups apart.*

MAYOR. Kotomtsev. I've got a bone to pick with you.

KOTOMTSEV. A bone? Boris Ivanovich, I'm all ears.

Some snickering from KOTOMTSEV'S SUBORDINATES.

MAYOR. A missing person. A soldier. He was on his way here by train and some of your lads picked him up.

KOTOMTSEV. Oh. Who could that have been, Boris Ivanovich?

MAYOR. Don't dick me about, Kotomtsev. I know what the score is. You had him, then you let him go; now he's wandering around town somewhere like a zombie. Just get hold of him again for me and we'll forget all about it.

KOTOMTSEV. Boris Ivanovich, I wish I could help you, but –

MAYOR. Just find him. You've got twenty-four hours. As of now. Clock's ticking.

KOTOMTSEV. Why? What's the big deal? He's just a bit fucked in the head, that's all –

MAYOR. You're the one who's fucked in the head! Shut up and get on with it!

KOTOMTSEV. All right. (*Under his breath.*) Keep your towel on.

KOTOMTSEV *stands up to leave.*

MAYOR. And no violence. Got it?

KOTOMTSEV *nods. He goes down the steps and leaves, his* ENTOURAGE *following him. The* MAYOR'S SUBORDI-NATES *expand to fill the fifth step.*

Aahhh. You know yesterday, I got that new secretary over to my office. We got completely hammered, now I can't remember a fucking thing. Think we might have shagged, but I'm not sure. It's all a bit of a furry blur.

One of his SUBORDINATES *stands up.*

SUBORDINATE. Oh, it's a constant problem, Boris Ivanovich. What did I stick where, did it actually happen, in the sense of where should I be sticking it anyway? It's all so unclear.

MAYOR. You find?

SUBORDINATE. No, in the sense that, with my wife, I can re-member every detail. But when I get a bit on the side – which is rare – complete opposite. You know how it is. I get so drunk to celebrate that...

The MAYOR *impatiently interrupts the* SUBORDINATE *with a wave of his hand.*

MAYOR. Oh, shut your face. (*To another* SUBORDINATE.) You there! Get off your arse and give us some steam, for Christ's sake!

Steam fills the stage.

Scene Eight

In the vodka bar. It's smoky and crowded. At a table sit TWO BARFLIES. *They have several empty glasses and a plate with the remains of some snacks in front of them.*

FIRST. Hey. Why weren't you at the station today?

SECOND. What station?

FIRST. The hero, you twat. How d'you get away with it? They herded all of us up at work. Every other person sent to the train station to give him his big welcome.

SECOND. I haven't been at work in three days.

FIRST. Oh, right.

SECOND. So, what's he like then? This hero?

FIRST. Great. Like fucking Rambo. Ripped, battle-scarred.

SECOND. Who gives a toss?

FIRST. Don't you get it? He's a hero. He can say or do anything he likes and no one can do a fucking thing about it.

SECOND. No one?

FIRST. He'll tell the truth, he'll cut through all the fucking bull-shit – because he's a hero.

SERGEY *and* ILYA *enter the bar.*

SECOND. Anything like this one?

FIRST. Nah! That fucking gayboy? Doesn't look like a soldier to me. Looks more like a student.

SERGEY (*shouting to the* WOMAN *at the bar*). Two lattes, please.

FIRST. Look at that. 'Two lattes, please.'

SECOND. Intellectuals.

FIRST. What's wrong with intellectuals? I'm an intellectual.

SECOND. Really?

FIRST. Well, I used to be, anyway. I think.

SECOND. 'Used-to-be's no fucking use. This is the here and now, mate. And now, you're not an intellectual, you're scum.

FIRST. Are you calling me scum?

SECOND. Yep. I am calling you scum. You, and me, and every-one else in this shithole.

FIRST. I'll smash your fucking face in.

SECOND. Fantastic. Where's that going to get you?

FIRST. Ahh, fuck it... let's have another drink.

The SECOND *gets up and staggers to the counter.*

SERGEY. ....So I was thinking, I should just up sticks and go
to Moscow. Why hang about here? But then – out of the
blue – our chief editor dies. This guy was pickled in
alcohol, like a donated organ, indestructible, we thought
he'd outlive everyone and everything – and suddenly, he's
gone and the whole newspaper's mine! For the first few
days I was so thrilled, all I could do was sit there. In my
new office, with a glass of vodka in my hand and my feet
up on the desk. Not even drinking it. Just sitting like that
for hours. I'd been dreaming of that moment since I was a
kid.

ILYA. I can't remember what I dreamt about when I was a
kid...

FIRST. Hang on. Didn't we just pour ourselves a drink?

SECOND. Yeah – we drank it.

FIRST. What the fuck's going on? We just poured ourselves a
drink, and now it's disappeared!

SECOND. Cos we drank it.

FIRST. I can't go on like this any more. This state of affairs.
I'm fundamentally opposed, I want to state my heartfelt
fucking opposition, d'you understand? It was here a second
ago, and now it's gone!

SECOND. We drank it, mate. Move on.

FIRST (*upset*). This isn't a life, it's like some sort of prison.
Fuck! Why does everything have to end? End so soon?
Why's life so cruel? Whose fault is it anyway?

SERGEY. Something funny happened to me today. I was writing something, on my computer, brand-new PC. Anyhow,
typing away and I type the word 'fuck'. And it underlines it

with the little red wiggly line – 'This word doesn't exist.' I thought, what the fuck's this? But then I remembered it was new. So I added 'fuck' to the dictionary. And then I realised that I'd taught my computer a swear word. And I felt ashamed. Dirty. Like I'd taught it to a child.

ILYA. I only use my computer for games. Shooters, *Doom*, stuff like that.

SERGEY. Yeah, but that's prehistoric, that's like fucking mammoth shit. The graphics you get now are amazing. D'you know the second *Half-Life* is out now? It took me a month to beat it, I was obsessed.

ILYA. Yeah. The first one was pretty cool, too.

SERGEY. Yeah, but the animation was shit. This one's mad – graphics are fucking Leonardo da Vinci. And get this. You get a pop-up helper on the second level, this girl. And when she winks at me – well, put it this way, she's not the only thing that pops up. Seriously, how sad is that? Because of a cartoon… But she's gorgeous.

Pause.

So did you see Natasha yet?

ILYA. Yeah.

Pause.

SERGEY. Hrmm… And so… are you… okay with everything?

ILYA. 'With everything'?

SERGEY. Well, you know… I suppose it's hard for women, nowadays… in terms of… being on her own, and…

SERGEY *doesn't finish because the* SECOND BARFLY *comes over.*

SECOND. Lads, you wouldn't have three roubles, would you? You know how it is. We're just a bit short.

SERGEY *gets out some change and gives it to the* SECOND.

Thanks, mate, you're a fucking legend. (*To* ILYA.) So what's with the outfit, son? Back from the wars or something? Fancy dress?

ILYA. Well, I suppose you could say, I just got back from the army, yeah.

SECOND. Great. Let's have a drink, then. Celebrate.

SERGEY. Excuse me. We are trying to have a conversation here?

SECOND. Oh, right you are. Got it. Won't bother you any more.

The SECOND *goes to the bar.*

SERGEY. Listen, you could live in my office for a bit. It's massive.

ILYA. Thanks.

The SECOND *returns to his table with two glasses of vodka. He sits down.*

FIRST. So what are we drinking to?

SECOND. To the – (*He indicates* ILYA *and* SERGEY *with his head.*) intellectuals.

They clink glasses and drink. ILYA *and* SERGEY *get up to leave. The* FIRST *gets up and staggers over to them.*

FIRST. Lads, listen, I hope we didn't offend you –

SERGEY. It's fine.

FIRST. – but who the fuck do you think we are? You think we're just fucking... alkies or something? We've got brains. We've got a conscience, we've got feelings. I mean, who the fuck do you think we are? We've got everything. D'you understand what I'm saying? (*To* SECOND.) Tolyan, I'm right, aren't I?

SECOND. Leave them alone, Petya.

FIRST. What? I haven't touched them yet.

SERGEY. Can I get past, please?

FIRST. No, you stay right there. I'm not finished yet.

The FIRST *grabs* SERGEY *by the collar of his jacket.*
SERGEY *fiercely shrugs him off.*

You wanna have a go, do you, you fucking ponce? I'll twat
you so hard! Thought you could give us five roubles then do
what the fuck you like?

SERGEY. Fuck. Off.

FIRST *punches* SERGEY *in the face.* SERGEY *punches him*
back. SECOND *gets up to go over to* FIRST *and as he does*
so, knocks the table over. ILYA *watches, dismayed.* TWO
POLICEMEN *enter, handcuff them all and lead them away.*

Scene Nine

The police station. KOTOMTSEV's *office.* KOTOMTSEV *and*
EFREMOV *sit reading. The* MAYOR's AIDE *comes in and*
KOTOMTSEV *looks up from his papers.*

KOTOMTSEV. Ah, there you are. You took your time.

AIDE (*indicating* EFREMOV). What's he doing here?

KOTOMTSEV. Don't worry about him. He's a deaf mute.

EFREMOV. I'm not.

KOTOMTSEV. Well, you might as well be.

AIDE. Nonetheless, I'd prefer that we talk alone.

KOTOMTSEV. Efremov. Go and powder your nose.

Grudgingly, EFREMOV *leaves.*

AIDE. I haven't got long. The Mayor thinks I'm at a campaign
meeting.

KOTOMTSEV. 'Campaign meeting.' That sounds important.
Should I be having one of them?

AIDE. No, I think your appeal lies in your accessibility. By the way…

The AIDE *puts down a package on the table.*

KOTOMTSEV. What's that?

AIDE. A small token of my… appreciation.

KOTOMTSEV *unwraps the package. It's an SS dagger.*
KOTOMTSEV *grabs it and bring the blade up to his face.*

KOTOMTSEV. SS Eighth Division. Blood and honour. The skull and the lily. Fuck, it's even got a serial number! It's actually fucking genuine!

AIDE. Naturally.

KOTOMTSEV. Well. Thank you. Thank you very much. That's very… nice of you.

AIDE. So where's this soldier then?

KOTOMTSEV. Kostya, Kostya. Slow down. It's always straight to the fucking with you. What I want to know is, why is everyone so interested in a shell-shocked gimp? Specifically old fart-arse?

Pause.

AIDE. Well, you might see a gimp – but everyone else sees a hero.

KOTOMTSEV (*dubiously*). A *hero*?

AIDE. So they say.

KOTOMTSEV *looks puzzled. The* AIDE *sighs.*

Look. Our town hasn't really had what you'd call a glorious history, has it? I mean, what's our claim to fame? A brick factory, a distillery, cholera every three years. Not much in the way of culture, either – I believe somebody once wrote the introduction to a textbook on intercranial surgery here. That's it. Not even the first chapter, just the intro.

KOTOMTSEV. Stop fucking whinging. We've got a very significant history.

AIDE. Well, cannery aside, we haven't much to be proud of. Until now. Now, suddenly, we have a hero; a prodigal son. A brave soul, lost in the purgatory of war, mortally damaged but somehow he survived, et cetera, and now he's come back home. It's a good story. 'Everyone forgot about him – *except* his home town.' The Mayor's no fool. Despite appearances. He'll be first in line. 'Welcome, my suffering son! We salute thee. Have a drink, have a HobNob. Here's some keys to a cushy flat. Or rather, here's the keys to a cushy flat we'll take back off you when the fuss dies down.' Doesn't matter. What matters is that the town did not forget. The town welcomes its son. And the town is the Mayor. And the Mayor is the father.

KOTOMTSEV. My God, it's enough to make you puke!

AIDE. Mawkish, but effective.

KOTOMTSEV. So that fat bastard wants a photo-op with this cripple?

AIDE. It's his best chance of being re-elected.

KOTOMTSEV. It's fucking diabolical! So what do I do?

AIDE. Well, obviously it would be a conflict of interests for me to advise you. But let's just say it might be wise of you to show your prisoner some leniency.

KOTOMTSEV. Leniency?

AIDE. And when you finally announce your candidacy, it might also be wise to have an endorsement of your own.

KOTOMTSEV (*sighs heavily*). All this strategising… If only I could fight old fat-arse man to man. In a field.

He picks up the dagger.

I'd make him squeal like a piggy. I'd start by cutting off his fat arse, then his belly, then his neck… No, actually, I'd start with his belly, and then his…

AIDE. Exactly. Politics is all about calculation. Like a game of chess, you could say.

KOTOMTSEV. I'm not a big fan of chess. Not really my 'thing'. You can go. Keep me posted on what that pig gets up to.

AIDE. Happy to be of service.

The AIDE *gets up and leaves.* KOTOMTSEV *waits a moment.*

KOTOMTSEV. Efremov! Bring in the gimp!

KOTOMTSEV *stands up and reluctantly puts the dagger away into a safe.* EFREMOV *brings in* ILYA.

Hey! How's it going, hero?

ILYA. Bit of a headache. Otherwise, okay.

KOTOMTSEV. Howsabout a hug for your Uncle Viktor?

KOTOMTSEV *goes over and gives* ILYA *a bear-hug.*

I won't cry. I'm a bloody man. But in my heart I feel fucking... joy. For you, son. You could have died a hundred times. But you did it. You came back. May you rest in peace.

ILYA. If we're going to be charged, can I –

KOTOMTSEV. Charged? For what? A little disagreement in a bar? You've simply been my guest here for a few hours. And now you're free. To stroll around town, free as a bird. And if I need you, I'm sure I'll find you. How does that sound?

ILYA. Okay.

KOTOMTSEV. I'll just hang on to your passport here, all right? Just in case.

ILYA. My passport? What if I need to leave town?

KOTOMTSEV. Well, we can discuss it then. For now, you just get plenty of rest, all right? Your town's been waiting for you. And so have I. And now you're home. D'you understand?

ILYA. Yes.

KOTOMTSEV. And don't forget. I greeted you like my own
son, didn't I? You won't forget that, will you?

ILYA *nods*.

Don't be a stranger…

ILYA *leaves*. EFREMOV *and another* POLICEMAN *poke
their heads around the door*.

EFREMOV. What was all that about?

KOTOMTSEV. Quick! Follow the gimp! Don't let him out of
your sight!

EFREMOV *vanishes*. KOTOMTSEV *addresses the other*
POLICEMAN.

You. You're going to the cells.

Scene Ten

SERGEY *sits in a cell with another* PRISONER.
KOTOMTSEV *stands*.

KOTOMTSEV. So. Been disgracing our local press then, have
we? Beating up alkies in bars?

SERGEY. I should thank you for your hospitality, Viktor
Viktorovich. It's been very illuminating, seeing your cells
from the inside.

KOTOMTSEV. Have fun, did you?

SERGEY. Picked up a bit of gossip. Which I might use later.

KOTOMTSEV. Oh yes. Talking of which, you can write this in
your little shitrag. 'Man Found Dead in Street.' True story.
They did some blood tests, turned out he'd drunk two and
half litres of vodka. That takes real determination. That's five
bottles –

SERGEY (*shrugging*). Well, it's not really *news*, is it...

KOTOMTSEV. No, but get this. He didn't die of the alcohol. He was killed while he was cycling home. Knocked down by a car, fifty yards from his front door. Two and a half litres of vodka inside him and the fucker still managed to cycle home. Incredible.

SERGEY. Great. I'll write it up in our column 'Regional Records: My Personal Best.'

KOTOMTSEV. Smartarse. You want to watch out *you* don't end up in 'Regional Records'.

SERGEY. Are you threatening me?

KOTOMTSEV. Absolutely. Now, you listen to me. I'm going to be needing your paper soon. You'll be supporting me at the elections.

SERGEY. We're independent...

KOTOMTSEV (*interrupting*). That's exactly what we need, independents. First off, we need to give your little rag a new name. Something more dynamic. Like... *The Sword and the Panther*. What do you think?

SERGEY (*smiling sourly*). Well, it's a little bit...

KOTOMTSEV. Your first task – announce a competition to design the best coat of arms for the town. And none of that arty-farty crap, soft-focus tin cans in green fields. We want armour, we want shining steel, we want the wind humming in our ears, we want... (*Calming down.*) You get the picture. That's all.

He nods to the GUARD, *who unlocks the cell.*

Now fuck off.

SEGREY. I still...

KOTOMTSEV. Before I change my mind!

SERGEY *hurriedly leaves*.

Scene Eleven

ILYA *walks along a dark street. An elderly man,* BABITSKY, *in an overcoat appears near him.* ILYA *doesn't notice him straightaway; he has stopped, puzzled, and is reading out the name of the street.*

ILYA. 'Democracy Street...'

BABITSKY. They just renamed it. Used to be called 'Communist Street'. Before that, 'Blood-Letting Street' – a doctor lived here, time of the Tsar, treated people with leeches. Are you here on leave?

ILYA. 'On leave'?

BABITSKY. I'm on leave, in a sense. Well, retired. On a pension for the rest of my life...

ILYA. Do I – [*unspoken: 'know you'*]?

BABITSKY. It's Lev. Lev Anatolievich Babitsky. Your old biology teacher. 'Fly Trap.' Remember?

ILYA. Lev Anatolievich?

BABITSKY. Sharpen up, Ilya. The paleontology club, 'Young Fossils'?

ILYA. 'Young Fossils'... Yes. Of course. I remember.

BABITSKY. There was you, there was Kostya, Natasha, little Sergey. Sergey's a journalist now, you know. And Kostya, well, let's say you wouldn't recognise him, he's certainly carved his own path in life...

ILYA. Lev Anatolievich –

BABITSKY. Yes?

ILYA. We used to play a game – 'Save Your Dinosaur'? We had to make speeches –

BABITSKY. Yes, in defence of your dinosaur...

ILYA. Yes, but I was always the mastodon. Why was I always that one?

BABITSKY. The mastodon's a very fine dinosaur.

ILYA. No, it isn't. It's the clumsiest, stupidest dinosaur. It just chews leaves all day. That's all it fucking does. Why was I always the clumsy stupid one? The vegetarian?

BABITSKY (*looking closely at* ILYA). Ilya, you look awful. It's a good thing I ran into you.

ILYA (*starting to walk on*). I'm fine.

BABITSKY. What's happened? Tell me.

ILYA. Nothing's happened.

BABITSKY. Something's happened. People are looking for you –

ILYA. Nobody wants to see me. And I don't want to see anyone.

BABITSKY (*keeping pace with* ILYA). No, Ilya, come on. You look exhausted. Come back to mine. I live on my own, nobody's going to bother you there. You can just rest.

A monster-like PLUMP WOMAN *comes up to them in high excitement.*

PLUMP WOMAN. Oh, I'm so glad I bumped into you! You're Ilya, aren't you?

ILYA *just looks at her.*

Yes, I clocked you straightaway. They've hung a banner with your face on it over my windows. I live inside your head – get it?

She approaches.

It's a joke! They put up a banner with you on it over my windows, and I live behind it. So it looks like I live inside your head. It's a joke. You're Ilya, aren't you? The hero.

ILYA. Hero?

PLUMP WOMAN. Listen, is it true you're going to be our mayor now? Is that right?

ILYA *looks confused.*

ILYA. Me?

PLUMP WOMAN. Well, what I want to know is, when are they going to stop turning the hot water off in the middle of winter? Eh?

ILYA. Water?

PLUMP WOMAN. Yes, water, water. We're living in the Stone Age here, we've got to heat it up in bloody tea urns. And they never clear up the snow in the front yard, the snow's piled up to here – (*She draws her hand across her throat to show the height of the snow banks.*)

BABITSKY (*interrupting*). Liza? It is Liza, isn't it? Liza – what's your surname again?

PLUMP WOMAN (*frightened*). Why? What you need my surname for? I'm talking about the snow banks, that's all I'm talking about…

BABITSKY. No, you were my student. Liza. I taught you. Remember? Didn't you have to repeat year five – ?

She looks at him suspiciously.

PLUMP WOMAN (*making a point of only addressing* ILYA). Well, all I'm saying is, when you're elected, don't forget about us. That's all I wanted to say. That's it. I've said what I wanted to say. Ta very much.

She hurriedly leaves.

ILYA. She said that she lives inside my head…

BABITSKY (*ignoring* ILYA). Ribbit… Ribbit… Ribbitovsky! That's it. Liza Ribbitovksy! She was a good kid, well, you all were… all my children were good. Shall we go? It's not far…

He takes ILYA *by the hand and leads him away.*

Scene Twelve

BABITSKY*'s flat.* ILYA *is standing, looking at the photos on the walls.* BABITSKY *comes in with a tray of bottles and glasses filled with different-coloured liquids.*

BABITSKY. And now, Ilya, I'm going to fix – you – up. Sit down.

ILYA. What is that?

BABITSKY. Well, it's like this. I've been a pensioner for a while now. And at first, I thought I was going to miss work, miss my students. But turns out, no, I don't – not at all: what I really enjoy doing is making medicinal infusions. It's like cooking, only, you don't use a cooker, you use... vodka.

ILYA. No, no – I mustn't drink alcohol.

BABITSKY. Me neither, me neither. Listen, this stuff isn't going to fog up your brain. It's going to make it function properly.

ILYA. No, really, it's not.

BABITSKY. I'm the biology teacher, remember? Although I must admit, I got a bit disillusioned with biology. I've started going to church in my old age, and where does God fit into biology? Can you believe it? An atheist all my life, and now, I'm a believer! Do you? Believe?

ILYA. I don't know. I don't think I'm... grown up enough. But really – I can't...

BABITSKY. Well, frankly, my dear Ilya, God doesn't give a damn whether you believe in him or not. Bottoms up.

ILYA. Well, maybe just a little... Thing is, on the train the other day...

BABITSKY. A medicinal dose. Practically alcohol-free. I make it with root of mandrake.

ILYA *freezes, the glass at his lips.*

I'm joking, dear boy, I'm joking! Buds of willow, mint and some other herb... forgotten its name... Just drink it.

ILYA *drinks. He puts the glass down and staggers.*

ILYA. But this is... pure... alcohol!

BABITSKY. No. Nothing's pure these days. Everything's polluted. I walk around this empty town, kicking rubbish.

Another BABITSKY *appears from the darkness, lifts* ILYA *under his arms and carefully sits him down on the sofa, sits next to him.*

SECOND BABITSKY. I would have died long ago, Ilyusha, if it weren't for this joke. Want to hear it?

BABITSKY. Two men have a bet. The first – what was he called? – well, anyway, the second... the second one was... dearie me, can you believe it? I've forgotten their names. Now it won't be funny any more.

THIRD BABITSKY (*appearing from the darkness*). Doesn't matter. Two people made a bet about our town. Whether there were one hundred good people in it or not. They gave out questionnaires, market research. Were there a hundred? No. There weren't. But were there ninety-nine?

ILYA. No?

THIRD BABITSKY. There weren't. But ninety-eight? Nope, there weren't ninety-eight either. Ninety-seven? Nah. Ninety?

SECOND BABITSKY. To cut to the chase, it got down to one person.

ILYA. Natasha?

BABITSKY. Fuck Natasha! I'm talking about me! Me! Only I was left. So here I am, left walking around, kicking rubbish around this empty town. So what if I weren't there? I've forgotten... then what? What??

SECOND BABITSKY. Then there wouldn't be a town. But who needs it? Who needs the town?

ILYA. I do?

THIRD BABITSKY (*counting all the while, like a metronome*). Eighty-four? No. Eighty-three? No.

SECOND BABITSKY. You don't need it. You ended up here by accident. Everyone ends up here by accident.

BABITSKY. Some come drawn by dappled dogs, some take the taxi with three drivers, and some skate here over the frozen river.

SECOND BABITSKY. And some come here by foot, like you.

ILYA. I came by train!

BABITSKY. Don't lie to your old teacher!

SECOND BABITSKY. He's the only one left.

THIRD BABITSKY. I counted down to one and that one person was me.

SECOND BABITSKY. And living on a life-long pension is no joke.

THIRD BABITSKY. So. There's my funny story. Now you've got to laugh.

SECOND BABITSKY. But don't laugh at your old teacher.

ILYA. Natasha!

BABITSKY. They've made an arse out of life. Now go to sleep.

ILYA. I've got to go to Natasha's!

The SECOND *and* THIRD BABITSKY *disappear.* ILYA *is left standing anxiously in the middle of the room.*

BABITSKY. What are you on about, Ilyusha? It's late. You can go in the morning. It's late. Sleep, go on.

Scene Thirteen

BABITSKY's *flat. Morning. The* MAYOR *is shaking* ILYA *awake.*

MAYOR. Up we get! I've packed your toothbrush, packed your towel. We off? Or do you want a bit of breakfast first?

ILYA. Who...?

> BABITSKY *comes in. He's carrying plastic bags full of food.*

BABITSKY. That's my towel. Put it back. He didn't have a towel – Did you take the navy-blue toothbrush?

MAYOR. The blue one? Yeah.

ILYA. What's going on?

MAYOR. Come on, son, chop-chop. We've got a proper bed for you at the compound.

BABITSKY. Boris Ivanovich, don't rush the lad. Let him eat some breakfast first.

MAYOR. Fine. Fair enough. I could do with some breakfast too. What did you get?

> *He comes over to* BABITSKY *and peers inside the bags.*

Christ. That's what you spent my money on? Why did you buy all *this* shit?

BABITSKY. It's nutritious, low-fat –

MAYOR. It's bloody bird food – We'll eat at mine. And have a wee snifter while we're at it. Right, son? You ready?

ILYA. For what?

BABITSKY. You're better off with Boris Ivanovich than me, Ilyusha.

MAYOR. Course you are. Keep eating this kind of crap, you'll grow a beak.

ILYA (*to* BABITSKY). Did you bring him here?

MAYOR. All right then, say *ciao* to old Fly Trap and let's get out of here.

ILYA. But I don't want to go anywhere!

BABITSKY. Give that towel back. It's mine.

MAYOR (*slowly*). What did you say?

BABITSKY. The towel. Please.

The MAYOR *pulls the towel out of the bag.*

MAYOR. Stuff it up your arse. I never thought, Lev Anatolievich, that I'd see the day you refused to spare me a towel. You were my teacher. Didn't you teach us all to be generous? To be Good Samaritans?

BABITSKY (*guiltily*). But I'm on a pension now.

MAYOR. Yes yes yes. Well, vote for me, anyhow. Right, let's go.

BABITSKY. I'm so pleased for you, Ilyusha. They'll take good care of you.

MAYOR. Anyone you want to see, we'll bring them to you. Anything you want. Just get a move on. I've got a policy meeting I've got to go to.

BABITSKY. And you'll see, it's for the best. Maybe I can come and see you sometimes?

MAYOR (*patting* ILYA *on the shoulder*). So? Can he? What do we say?

Pause.

ILYA. Okay.

They leave. EFREMOV, *who has been watching, makes a phone call.*

Scene Fourteen

KOTOMTSEV *stares at his phone in horror. He dials another number quickly.*

KOTOMTSEV. Kostya – my man just called me. That fat-arse got the cripple! He's taken him to the compound!

The MAYOR*'s* AIDE *appears, taking the call.*

AIDE. Yes, I know. That was careless of you.

KOTOMTSEV. It wasn't my fault. That dessicated old fuck of a teacher served him up on a plate!

AIDE. Oh, well – not to worry.

KOTOMTSEV. Not to worry?! You said – be lenient, you said! I had him in my hands and I let him go! So you're the one who should worry because, I swear –

AIDE. Trust me, Viktor Viktorovich. There's no need for concern. I have everything in hand.

KOTOMTSEV. You better had, Kostya, or you'll answer to Delilah!

He puts the phone down. He looks at his sword.

What? What did you say?

He picks up the sword, stares at it.

Yes – you're right. Of course you are. It'll be soon, my darling. It'll be soon...

Scene Fifteen

A meeting at the MAYOR*'s office. At the table sit the*
MAYOR'S OFFICIALS, KOTOMTSEV, SERGEY *and the*
MAYOR *with his* AIDE.

MAYOR. Come on! Where are all the brilliant new policy
ideas! This is meant to be a brainstorming session, I'm not
even getting a light fucking drizzle! Viktor Viktorovich!
What are you smirking at? Don't tell me you're actually
thinking? Go on. Stand up and tell everyone what's limping
through your tiny mind.

KOTOMTSEV. Everything's going well in all our departments.
And we are, as usual, making it our priority to monitor and
safeguard the security of our citizens.

MAYOR (*to* SERGEY). Okay. So here's what you write. 'At
the Mayor's electoral policy meeting, the Chief of Police
stood up and bleated like a homesick goat.'

KOTOMTSEV. Boris Ivanovich!

MAYOR. Well, has someone – anyone – please, got something
of substance to say on the matter? Vassiliev?

VASSILIEV *gets up with alacrity.*

VASSILIEV. Can I help?

MAYOR. What's the time?

VASSILIEV. Four o'clock.

MAYOR. You! Saveliev!

SAVELIEV *stands up eagerly.*

SAVELIEV. Yessir.

MAYOR. Have you got a brilliant new policy idea?

SAVELIEV. Certainly have, sir.

MAYOR. Hit me with it!

SAVELIEV. We should convert the town square into a skating rink for the general public. And then everyone'll bring their children out to skate at the weekends.

MAYOR. That it?

SAVELIEV. That's it for now, yes.

The MAYOR *slumps, depressed.*

MAYOR. How many children have you got, Saveliev?

SAVELIEV. Just my little Mashka.

MAYOR. Where's number two? And three? Are you firing blanks, man? I just don't get why the public aren't breeding. Where are the demographic booms? Where the hell is all that?

SAVELIEV (*shrugging his shoulders helplessly*). Well, it's winter, you know. It's cold...

MAYOR (*tiredly*). Christ... Sit down, Saveliev. 'He's cold...' You get right on my tits, you know that? Listen. Try and get this into your heads. I can't stand up there tomorrow without a single new policy!

KOTOMTSEV *cannot contain his smirk.*

KOTOMTSEV. But you do have the 'hero', Boris Ivanovich.

The MAYOR *eyes him suspiciously.*

MAYOR. You know, Viktor Viktorovich, I'm beginning to worry about our police force. I've got a feeling it could do with some downsizing. What do you think?

KOTOMTSEV. What do I think?

MAYOR. Haven't you got anything to say?

KOTOMTSEV. Sorry, do you want me to say something?

MAYOR. Ah, go fuck yourselves, the lot of you! (*To* SERGEY.) Er – excuse me. What exactly are you scribbling down in your little notebook? That's the fourth time today. There hasn't been a single word of any substance and you keep beavering away.

SERGEY. I don't have to write.

MAYOR (*mimicking him*). 'I don't have to write.' So don't bloody write then!

SERGEY *exaggeratedly puts the notebook away.*

You know, I just thought of a policy. We make your paper municipal.

SERGEY. What for?

MAYOR (*repeating slowly and clearly*). Municipal. Of course, it'll need a new name.

KOTOMTSEV. Er – Boris Ivanovich – I think there are already plans to rename the paper. Aren't there?

MAYOR. Rename it to what?

KOTOMTSEV *waggles his eyebrows suggestively to* SERGEY.

SERGEY (*reluctantly*). *The Sword and the Panther.*

MAYOR. The sword and the fucking what?? No no no. We'll call it *The Departmental News.* You'll cover all the dull shit we do. Demographics, ice rinks in the square, all that sort of crap. Got it?

SERGEY. We have shareholders, it's not that simple…

MAYOR. Shareholders invest in the town. And we invest in the shareholders. Everyone invests in everyone. That's why you'll do what I say and stop being a pain in the arse. Clear? Everyone?

SAVELIEV (*standing up*). Crystal.

MAYOR. Vassiliev. Any notes? Anything further to add?

VASSILIEV. Eight minutes past four. Nothing further to add.

SERGEY *gets up from his seat.*

SERGEY. Boris Ivanovich, this is completely –

Everyone stares at him. The MAYOR *gives* SERGEY *a withering look.*

– fine. No problem at all. *The Departmental News* – good name, just... a bit bland. What about *The Departmental Messenger*?

Pause.

MAYOR. Better, much better. First class. Four stars. Viktor Viktorovich? Any objections or... crap you want to bring up?

KOTOMTSEV. What about, Boris Ivanovich? It all seems perfectly clear to me.

MAYOR (*with mock relief*). Well, thank God for that! There I was thinking I'd have to put a rocket under all your useless arses.

Vassiliev?

VASSILIEV. Ten past four, exactly.

MAYOR (*rubbing his hands together*). Ten past four. Well. Splendid!

Everyone gets up and leaves – KOTOMTSEV *giving* SERGEY *a dirty look on the way out. Only* SERGEY *and the* AIDE *remain. Suddenly,* SERGEY *pounds the table.*

SERGEY. Fuck, fuck, fuck!

The AIDE *coolly lights a cigarette and eyes him.*

Scene Sixteen

Inside the MAYOR*'s compound,* ILYA *watches television. Two* GUARDS *bring* NATASHA *in.*

NATASHA. Ilya, what the hell's going on?

ILYA. I'm sorry, they don't seem to want me to leave this place.

NATASHA. Fine, so they just come and march me out of my house?

ILYA. Where's Ivan?

NATASHA. He's at home.

ILYA. What, by himself?

NATASHA. No.

Pause.

ILYA. My head's stopped hurting. For the first time in ages.

NATASHA. That's good…

ILYA. Listen… yesterday… I know I left… sort of suddenly –

NATASHA. It doesn't matter –

ILYA (*interrupting*). No but it does, because – I've been able to think about it, and I don't want much, but –

Pause.

I just want to see him sometimes. Take him out, maybe, every so often, or –

NATASHA. No, Ilya, listen –

ILYA. No, no, no, I know we can't change what happened between us.

NATASHA. Ilya, that's not –

ILYA. But with Ivan – it's different. He shouldn't have to –

NATASHA. Ilya, you're not listening to me!

ILYA. He shouldn't have to suffer just because of our mistakes, he should be able to see –

NATASHA. Ilya, STOP. Just stop, be quiet for a second and listen.

Pause.

Ilya. You're dead.

Pause.

ILYA (*shocked*). What?

NATASHA. He thinks... I *told* him... that you died.

ILYA *puts his hand to his head.*

ILYA. What... What did you just say?

NATASHA. I told him you were dead.

Pause.

He can't have two fathers, Ilya. It's too confusing for him.

Pause.

And anyway we wouldn't have stayed together. Why put all those questions in his head? Why make him feel guilty for something that isn't his fault? He didn't do anything wrong. We were the ones who did things wrong.

Pause.

Okay then, it's *me* who did everything wrong. Is it easier for you to think that? Easier to cope? But Ilya, if you'd really cared about us – you could have got out of being con-scripted. You didn't even ask if I *wanted* you to stay. We could have come up with something, bribed somebody... But no, you did what you were told because that's what you've been taught. The state says we're at war so you go to war. Well, I was taught the same things as you, I know what 'duty' means, but after he was born, I suddenly understood – there is no state. Fuck the state. The state's got nothing to do with me and him. But that's what you chose, Ilya. So what claim do you have on us now?

ILYA. Do you want me to say something?

NATASHA. No. You don't need to say anything. I just want you to understand...

ILYA. I do.

Pause.

NATASHA. You're a good friend, Ilya. Strong. The mastodon.

ILYA. Yeah. The mastodon.

Pause.

NATASHA. There's posters of you everywhere. They're saying you're a hero.

Pause.

We'll need to talk about the divorce. But it can wait till summer, if you like. When it's a bit warmer. Okay?

ILYA. Okay. We'll talk in the summer.

NATASHA *exits, leaving* ILYA *alone.*

Scene Seventeen

The spacious office of the MAYOR. *It's morning.* ILYA *sits at the* MAYOR'*s desk. He's reading through some papers. The* AIDE *stands next to him, waiting for* ILYA *to finish reading. There is the sound of a toilet flushing. Behind the desk, a little concealed door opens and the* MAYOR *comes out. He's wearing a dressing gown and flip-flops and is holding a newspaper. He stops and looks at* ILYA.

MAYOR. And now, I'm going to die.

AIDE. It just so happens I've got some aspirin on me.

He goes over to the MAYOR *and offers him the tablets. The* MAYOR *waves him away.*

MAYOR. Bugger off with your chemicals.

The MAYOR *is holding an empty bottle of vodka. The* AIDE *takes it off him.*

AIDE (*firmly*). No more vodka.

MAYOR. Why? Why shouldn't I drink vodka?

AIDE (*reproachfully*). Boris Ivanovich.

MAYOR. I'm fed up with the lot of you. You're all bores. You included.

ILYA (*looks up from the papers*). Okay. I've finished reading it. What is it?

AIDE. It's your speech.

ILYA. My *speech*?

MAYOR. Anyway, I thought we still had a bit left over, didn't we? Snifter?

AIDE (*speaking slowly and clearly*). After. The. Press. Conference. Is that clear?

ILYA. What do you mean, my speech? It says here that I took Grozny. I've never been to Grozny. Our unit was based near Nazran. Thirty kilometres away.

AIDE. Not important. What's important is that everyone understands you respect and support the political line upheld by the head of our administration.

MAYOR (*confidentially*). Son... listen to me, son...

He lowers himself into an armchair, with difficulty.

ILYA. I'm listening.

MAYOR. Do me a favour and nip down to reception, would you? There's a minibar there...

AIDE. Boris Ivanovich, please! You don't seem to understand that whether you are elected for a third term or not is dependent on you getting through this press conference without passing out! Why are you determined to get drunk?

MAYOR. Okay, okay, just don't shout. My head might explode.

AIDE. I just can't bear it any more. How many times do I have to tell you –

MAYOR (*suddenly rising from the armchair*). Shut up!! Who the fuck do you think you are?! Telling me what to do? If I want to drink, I'll fucking drink! Now go to the bar!

AIDE. Boris Ivanovich...

MAYOR. I said, go to the bar, and get me a fucking drink!

AIDE. I'm going.

MAYOR. Now!

AIDE (*bitterly*). Fine.

The AIDE leaves. The MAYOR clutches at his heart, sinks limply back down into the armchair.

MAYOR (*speaking more and more quietly as he gets weaker and weaker*). They're going to kill me. These people. You think it works, treating them like human beings? I've tried. The first time I ran for mayor, I thought, unless I completely fuck things up, in four years we'll have a garden city here. I thought, I'll be the kindest, gentlest... But do they understand kindness, these people? No. All they understand is force, brute fucking force. It's a Russian thing...

The AIDE comes back with a shot of vodka in his hand. He gives it to the MAYOR. The MAYOR takes it, and squints at it critically, holding it up against the light.

(*Peevishly.*) Like you've milked a mouse. Well. Your health.

AIDE (*bitterly*). No thanks. To yours.

The MAYOR downs it and then covers himself with the newspaper as if going back to bed.

(*To ILYA, in a businesslike tone.*) So. Today we launch the election. There'll be lots of fun and games, and vodka distributed free of charge. Am I right, Boris Ivanovich?

A muffled groan is heard from under the newspaper.

Now, at about one o'clock, you're going to read out this
speech. Better still, learn it off by heart on the way there.
You'll be taken to the town square; people'll be gathered
waiting for you. After the speech, Boris Ivanovich will come
out, and you'll both sing a song together.

ILYA. I can't sing.

MAYOR (*from under the newspaper*). Neither can I.

AIDE. Neither can he. Doesn't matter. Just open and shut your
mouths.

MAYOR. Enthusiastically.

AIDE. Then, the climax: you'll be given the keys to the town.

MAYOR (*interested*). Are there actually keys?

AIDE. Yes. But they're symbolic.

MAYOR. What do they open?

AIDE. Nothing. They're symbolic.

MAYOR. Well, what's the fucking point of that?

AIDE. It means he's a Freeman of the town. Then Boris
Ivanovich will give you the keys to a flat.

MAYOR. But they don't open it?

AIDE. No, they do, they're just keys.

MAYOR. I'm confused.

AIDE. After that, you thank Boris Ivanovich. You say everyone
turned their backs on you, except your beloved home town.
And that all these years all you wanted was to come back
here. And now you're very happy.

MAYOR. Five minutes of bullshit and you've got the keys to a
flat. Job well done.

ILYA. Where's this flat going to be?

MAYOR. In the centre.

ILYA. I already lived in the centre.

MAYOR. Oh, boohoo! You want to live in the outskirts?
There's still some condemned tower blocks there if you
really want, that good enough for you?

ILYA. I already lived in the tower blocks.

MAYOR (*in a weak, pitiful voice from under the newspaper*).
I can't stand this. I can't stand this any more. Take him
away.

AIDE. Ilya, trust us, we're on your side. The flat will be very
nice, you'll like it. Boris Ivanovich only wants the best for
you. Oh, and by the way. A girl will come up to you when
you're standing on the rostrum. She's the winner of our local
beauty contest. She'll be standing next to you.

MAYOR. Don't grab her arse.

ILYA. I'll try not to.

AIDE. And don't forget to smile. Do you know how to smile?
Give it a go.

ILYA *smiles. The* MAYOR *peers from round his newspaper
with interest.*

Oh dear...

MAYOR. ....My grandfather smiled like that. Just before he
died.

AIDE. Better not. The girl can smile for the pair of them.

MAYOR. And I'll muddle through on my own somehow.

The MAYOR *suddenly throws the newspaper off him and
springs up, full of life.*

Okay, enough chat. We need to live, love and be happy. Let's
get this show on the road.

AIDE. Might I respectfully suggest you wear something more
appropriate?

MAYOR. Oh yes. I knew I'd forgotten something. So who's
taking the crip – the hero to the square?

AIDE. We've got a police escort waiting. We'll follow you down.

The MAYOR *comes up to* ILYA, *kisses him on the cheeks three times. Inspects his face.*

MAYOR (*to* ILYA). Face like a slapped arse. Cheer up, it might never happen. We all love you. Remember that.

He leaves, murmuring to himself.

All the king's horses and all the king's men... So now then... first, minibar, then, public. Not bad, not bad...

The MAYOR *leaves. The* AIDE *waits for the* MAYOR *to clear.*

ILYA. So what happens next?

KOTOMTSEV *enters.*

KOTOMTSEV. I'm what happens next.

ILYA *turns to him, surprised.*

You've disappointed me, Ilya.

ILYA. Have I?

KOTOMTSEV. Didn't I greet you like my own son? Didn't I bring you into my own house and feed you, give you a bed and a roof over your head for the night?

ILYA. You mean the cells?

KOTOMTSEV. You've offended me, Ilya. Sucking up to that old fat-arse. You've deeply fucking offended me. In fact, I don't know how I'm going to live with this offence. If this was two hundred years ago, I'd start by cutting off your head, then I'd drag your body to the main square so that everybody could spit on it when they walked past, and then, and only then, would I consider my honour, in some small way, to be restored. That's how offended I am.

ILYA. I'm sorry, I didn't mean to...

AIDE. But there is a way to iron all this out. Isn't that right, Viktor Viktorovich?

KOTOMTSEV (*with deep hatred*). A pig isn't there to give
  orders. A pig is there to be slaughtered, when the time is
  ripe.

AIDE (*to* ILYA). He's talking about the Mayor.

KOTOMTSEV. I hate the fucking pig...

AIDE. Viktor Viktorovich, did you hear what I said?

KOTOMTSEV. No. I didn't hear what you fucking said.

AIDE. I said that Ilya would like to make it up with you.

ILYA. Yes, I would really...

KOTOMTSEV. Great. Well, explain it all to him then.

AIDE. So, listen, Ilya. Here's a copy of the speech.

ILYA. I've already got a copy.

KOTOMTSEV. And you can stuff *that* speech up the Mayor's
  arse.

AIDE. In other words, you won't be needing that one. This
  speech says that mayors like Boris Ivanovich –

KOTOMTSEV. – should be cut up. Into cubes, the bastard, and
  then again, and again, into smaller, and smaller pieces until –

AIDE. Well, you get the gist. And then, it concludes that, naturally, people like Viktor Viktorovich here –

KOTOMTSEV. – will restore truth and justice to this town.
  According to the ancient Russian order of chivalry.

AIDE. Or words to that effect. Got it?

ILYA. Yes... er, I think so...

AIDE. Nothing to be frightened of. You just need to read it out.
  All of it. People need to know the truth about the Mayor.
  And now, they will.

KOTOMTSEV. And I'll present you with a sabre that belonged
  to Khagan, Prince of Khazaria. It's a fake, of course, but as
  fakes go, not half bad. Steel with a high carbon count,
  engraving running one third of the length from the hilt –

AIDE. Don't worry, you'll still get the flat – just later, when he's mayor.

KOTOMTSEV. – and when it's hot, enough dew condenses on the blade for two lightly armed cavalrymen to quench their thirst. So – (*To* ILYA.) Are you with us?

ILYA *rubs his head.*

You promised. Remember?

ILYA. Yes.

KOTOMTSEV. And then I'll give you your passport back. And we'll celebrate. With the sword. We'll toast the sabre.

AIDE. Talking of weapons. We were just given a pair of Solingen daggers as a gift. By our twin town in Germany.

KOTOMTSEV. Solingen daggers!? As a gift??

AIDE. Yes. It's a little distasteful. That's why the Mayor sent them to your boys – to melt them down.

KOTOMTSEV. Melt them down? When??

AIDE. Oh, about… half an hour ago.

KOTOMTSEV. Right. You wait there. Don't move. Make sure he learns the speech.

KOTOMTSEV *hurries out of the room, already on his phone.*

(*On his phone.*) Efremov! Pick up your phone! The daggers!

He is gone.

AIDE. Okay. You need to come with me.

ILYA. He told us not to move.

AIDE. Well, he's an idiot.

ILYA. I thought you were working for him?

AIDE. I am. And for the Mayor.

ILYA. Both of them?

AIDE. Yes. It's all rather thrilling, isn't it?

Plates spinning... dice rolling... everything in motion... but in which direction, Ilya?

ILYA. I don't know.

AIDE. In the most interesting direction possible. And it's not over yet.

They leave.

Scene Eighteen

The AIDE *and* ILYA *in an abandoned schoolroom. A broken blackboard lies on the floor, desks jumbled up into a pile, old exercise books on the floor, the lino torn up in places, and gaps in the glass in the windows, where the snow has come through and piled up inside.*

ILYA. Why've you brought me here?

AIDE. Don't you remember? Room fifteen.

Pause.

ILYA. The dinosaur club.

The AIDE *arches his arms and makes the squawking noise of a pterodactyl.* ILYA *turns to him.*

Kostya?

The AIDE *smiles.*

I remember you now. Kostya. You were the pterodactyl.

AIDE. Yes. Shame to be the first bird to die out. I always hated school.

ILYA. I'm sorry – I didn't recognise you. You've really changed.

AIDE. I like to think that I've evolved. You haven't changed at all. It's only you, the dinosaurs, that didn't evolve.

The door opens, SERGEY *comes in.*

SERGEY. That's why they died out. Evolve or die. That's what we were taught. Isn't it?

ILYA *turns to* SERGEY *in confusion.* SERGEY *is looking around the room.*

Room fifteen. Look at the state of it. You know they're going to knock all this down? The place where we were taught. They do what the hell they like –

ILYA. I don't know why I came back. Nothing makes sense any more. She told him I was dead. My son thinks I'm dead. Maybe I am.

SERGEY. But you have a choice, Ilya. You can choose to die. Or you can choose to evolve. But you do have to choose.

ILYA (*blankly*). Choose between what?

SERGEY. Kotomtsev or the Mayor, the Mayor or Kotomtsev. What's it going to be?

ILYA. But I don't want to choose anyone!

SERGEY. Okay.

ILYA. I came here to… to see Natasha. To see my son. To kill some time, go to the river. Sit and talk shit with you. Where else am I going to go?

SERGEY. Exactly.

ILYA. I don't have anywhere else. Just this place. (*He looks around.*) And look at it.

SERGEY. Yes, but there's us –

ILYA. I know, that's what I said.

SERGEY. No, I mean you could choose us. You could support us – at the elections. Or, more specifically, me.

ILYA *silently absorbs this.*

The people need to hear someone speak the truth. Two monsters are devouring our town, two tyrants who deserve nothing better than immediate exile. We need to show them, we're not as weak as they think we are. I've got a newspaper. And I've got Kostya. And if you support me – Ilya, you've got to do it. I mean, what do you want out of life?

ILYA. I want the headaches to stop.

SERGEY. What else?

ILYA. I want everything to go back, like it was before.

SERGEY. But it can't go back. It can only get better, or worse.

ILYA. Better, then.

SERGEY. Then you have to choose. You have to choose us.

ILYA (*becoming subdued*). You think you stand a chance?

SERGEY. If you read this speech out, yes. (*He hands* ILYA *the speech.*) Just take a look at it. Ilya, we can run this town, we can run it the way it should be run. Just read it. It's brilliant, it's full of the stuff people want to hear, loads of stuff about a 'free town' and a 'prosperous future', and blah blah blah.

ILYA. Why not just read it yourself?

SERGEY. Because you're a hero. You think you're weak but you're not, you're strong. You were always stronger than any of us. You've been out there fighting for your country, you sacrificed everything –

ILYA. So did a lot of people. What's so special about me?

SERGEY. What's so special about you? (*He looks at* ILYA.) You're Ilya. The bravest and strongest of all of us. You're the mastodon!

A pause as ILYA *realises what this means.*

ILYA. Yes. I'm the mastodon.

SERGEY. ...So, Ilya, we haven't got long. I'm not forcing you. What do you think? Are you with us?

He offers ILYA *the speech. A long pause and then* ILYA, *without enthusiasm, takes it.*

I knew you wouldn't let me down. When it gets to the speeches, you read this out. Read it properly, don't skip anything. And democracy will triumph.

The AIDE *stifles a snigger with a cough.* SERGEY *shoots him a beady look.*

ILYA. Can I go now?

AIDE. I'll take him.

SERGEY. Fine. (*To* ILYA.) So I'll see you at the town square, Ilya.

(*As* ILYA *leaves.*) Everything's going to be okay, Ilya. Don't worry. You'll see.

Scene Nineteen

A red carpet stretches to a podium. Many REVELLERS *fill the town square, including a* BAND.

On the podium, the MAYOR *stands by a micophone, a* PRETTY GIRL *at his side who is carrying a tray of vodka shots.*

There is great hubbub – much waving of flags and jollity. All of it stops suddenly, everyone frozen.

ILYA *enters and observes them.*

Everything starts up again. The MAYOR *sees* ILYA.

MAYOR. Ah, here he is! Welcome, my son!

The CROWD *turns to see him, all cheering. Photographs are taken.*

SERGEY *enters behing* ILYA, *with his* STAFF PHOTOGRAPHER. *On the podium, the* AIDE *appears.*

Come on, don't be shy! Come up to the stage!

ILYA *steps forward. He is intercepted by a* WOMAN IN A BERET.

WOMAN IN BERET. All right, hero, how's it going?

Everyone else freezes again.

You know what? Come and check us out. We just opened – striptease club, where the children's library used to be. We've got ten girls, do a bit myself as well. We'll give you a discount. First two beers for free. No grabbing arse though. We're respectable. But we'll think up something tasty for you.

She takes a long slug from her glass.

I mean, you can grab *my* arse, if you like. No really, help yourself. Bet it's been ages, hasn't it it – and I've always liked shell-shocked blokes. My first husband was like that. One of those faces, you know, his gob half-open, like 'What the hell's going on?' Want me to come and find you after your speech?

The CROWD *unfreezes.* KOTOMTSEV *joins the* MAYOR *on the podium.*

KOTOMTSEV. That's it. Just a little bit further, hero.

MAYOR. Everybody make way for the hero!

ILYA *takes a few more steps. A short, thin* ELDERLY MAN, *with piercing eyes, comes up to* ILYA. *He has medals pinned to his jacket.*

ELDERLY MAN. So, soldier. Where were you wounded?

The CROWD *freezes.*

ILYA *indicates his head. The* ELDERLY MAN *takes hold of his head and leans* ILYA *towards him so he can inspect the back of his head.*

Ooh, yes, that's nasty, quite a smack. Bit deeper and it would have been curtains for you. Have a look at what they did to me.

The ELDERLY MAN *shows* ILYA *the back of his head, parting his hair.*

What do you think of that, eh? No dog's dick, is it, an aerial bomb – serious stuff. And it bloody throbs, your skull. Doesn't it? I know. So does mine. That's for life, that is. And you know what else?

The ELDERLY MAN *beckons* ILYA *closer in.* ILYA *bends down.*

(*Without switching to a whisper.*) All of these jokers here – they know fuck all about war! Fuck all! They didn't have a fucking shell fall on their bonces! Just you and me. We're the only ones who really know what it's like! Got it?

ILYA *nods.*

So just you go up there and show them, you tell them how it really is.

The CROWD *unfreezes. They move closer and closer in on* ILYA.

The FIRST BARFLY *comes up to* ILYA, *takes his coat off as if preparing to start a fight, but instead, makes a few dance-like moves and falls back into the* CROWD. *Everyone claps.*

MAYOR. All right, all right, don't crowd the lad. (*To the* PRETTY GIRL.) Go and get him.

The PRETTY GIRL *extends her hand and helps* ILYA *up to the podium.*

SERGEY *follows them up with his* PHOTOGRAPHER.

SERGEY. Okay, turn this way please, want to get your faces, that's it –

ILYA *has his photo taken with the* PRETTY GIRL.

The MAYOR *steps in, pointing to himself.*

MAYOR. One of us. One of us.

KOTOMTSEV *intercepts, grabbing* ILYA *by the shoulders and speaking into the microphone.*

KOTOMTSEV (*abruptly*). We, the organs of justice and defence, hand over our hero into the arms of the father of our town!

Photos are taken.

We were the ones who kept you in health, in our thoughts and in our prayers! And now, you're reunited with us once more.

The CROWD *claps.*

MAYOR (*in an undertone*). Kotomtsev, what the hell are you playing at?! (*Opening his arms wide again, raising his voice.*) Welcome back, my son!

The CROWD *claps.*

We've all been waiting for you!

The CROWD *claps.*

We don't become heroes, we die heroes. And the most heroic hero is the hero who returns to his motherland. Because only in his motherland will he be truly recognised as a hero. Where else? That's why we're all gathered here today, for you, my son. Hip hip – hooray! (*He starts to sing.*) For he's a jolly good fellow...

The CROWD *claps.*

And now, everybody – let the feast begin. I mean, beg pardon, let the speech begin. Our hero wants to make a speech.

The CROWD *claps. The* PRETTY GIRL *steps forward. The* MAYOR *takes a glass off her tray.*

AIDE. What about the toast?

CROWD (*a cheer*). Yes, a toast!!

MAYOR. And our last little formality – a toast!

He passes a glass to ILYA. ILYA *does not take it.*

(*To* ILYA.) Come on, son, we've got to have a toast together. What're you playing silly buggers for?

(To CROWD.) He's just come back from the valley of death
and he doesn't even need a drink! But everyone wants to celebrate with you!

KOTOMTSEV. Come on – have a drink!

CROWD *(chanting).* Drink, drink, drink!

At the back of the CROWD, NATASHA *enters.* BABITSKY
watches from the sidelines.

SERGEY. Yes, go on, Ilya – have a drink. The speech will flow
more easily.

ILYA *accepts the glass, silently.*

The CROWD *cheers.* ILYA *stares at the glass. He takes out
the three speeches and looks at them.*

KOTOMTSEV. What's all that? Kostya?

MAYOR. Kostya – Our speech wasn't that long, was it?

ILYA *looks up and sees* NATASHA.

The CROWD *hushes and follows his gaze, to* NATASHA.

ILYA *raises his glass to her… and drinks.*

As he finishes his glass the CROWD *goes wild, bursting into
applause. The* MAYOR *swigs his own glass, grabs* ILYA*'s
glass, and smashes both empty glasses to the ground as hard
as he can.*

Ladies and gentlemen – he's back!!

The CROWD *bursts into a joyful roar. A 'FIRST ILYA'
appears behind him and takes a sheet, then a SECOND
ILYA appears and takes a sheet, and then, finally, a THIRD.
ILYA himself stands, looking lost. He looks out at the
CROWD, confused.*

Each ILYA *is possessed by the character of the speech that
they are holding. Thus, the FIRST ILYA is 'MAYORlike' in
character; the SECOND like KOTOMTSEV; the THIRD
like SERGEY.*

FIRST ILYA. What does it say?

The CROWD *freezes. Looking narrowly at the text, the* FIRST ILYA *winces.*

'I promise to protect the interests of my electorate.' Well – I promise that all the time, don't I?

SECOND ILYA (*looking at his speech, displeased*). Fuck! What's this!

'I guarantee you a calm and steady life.' I'll show you a steady life, mate. You'll be steady when you're stuck on the end of my sword.

THIRD ILYA (*looking at his speech*). 'Freedom of speech and free will.' (*He harrumphs sarcastically.*) Not sure about *that*.

FIRST ILYA (*to* SECOND *and* THIRD). Couldn't they have written this better? I'll fire the fuckers. I'll teach them to write speeches...

SECOND ILYA (*to* FIRST *and* THIRD). That's fucking bad writing, that is. It's porridge. A speech has got to be... muscular! A speech has got to make people come out of the trenches and march forward, onwards and upwards. I need a speech that will make their blood boil and hearts sing!

THIRD ILYA (*to* FIRST *and* SECOND). I think some things should be stressed more and some stressed less. In any case, it needs a rewrite. There's no vitality to it.

All three turn to ILYA.

FIRST ILYA. Do you like this speech?

ILYA *is silent.*

THIRD ILYA. Ilya? What do you think of it?

ILYA *is silent.*

SECOND ILYA. Answer me like a man. Like a warrior, boy.

ILYA *is silent.*

FIRST ILYA (*to* SECOND *and* THIRD). What are we going to do with him? He's away with the fairies.

SECOND ILYA (*to* FIRST *and* THIRD). He needs a good smack on the head. Do him a power of good.

THIRD ILYA (*to* FIRST *and* SECOND). No, no, no. He needs a different approach.

FIRST ILYA *comes up to* ILYA.

FIRST ILYA. Look at these people, Ilya. A whole town square full of people, all waiting to hear what you're going to say. You know lots of them, some of them very well, you love a few of them, you're fond of others. What are you going to say to all of them now?

SECOND ILYA *comes up to* ILYA.

SECOND ILYA. Look at these people. You can say whatever you like. They're used to it. In fact, they're actually *expecting* you to spout a load of complete fucking rubbish. Are you happy about that?

THIRD ILYA *comes up to* ILYA.

THIRD ILYA. Look at these people. No, really look at them, properly. What do you see?

SECOND ILYA. They look like a blanket. A big grey blanket. Like the blanket I had in the army. It had a number sewn onto it.

FIRST ILYA. They look like gravel. The gravel I walked on every day on my way to school.

THIRD ILYA. Look at these people. They don't know anything about life.

FIRST ILYA. They're happy. They look at you and they think they're lucky.

SECOND ILYA. You're their hero.

THIRD ILYA. A hero arrives bringing victory. A hero brings peace. A hero leads the way. A hero brings hope.

FIRST ILYA. Help them.

SECOND ILYA. Do something for them.

THIRD ILYA. Promise them something, at least.

ILYA *is silent, looking at each of them.*

FIRST ILYA. Read it. They're waiting for your speech.

SECOND ILYA. Sock it to them. Give it a good kick up the arse.

THIRD ILYA. Don't try and make them like you. Just be yourself, they'll believe you.

FIRST ILYA. Come on, son.

SECOND ILYA. Go for it, soldier.

THIRD ILYA. You'll make it, my friend. We believe in you.

The CROWD *unfreezes, but they are hushed and confused. Some laugh.*

MAYOR. Come on, son, what's wrong with you? Read the speech.

KOTOMTSEV. Yes, come on, hero – read the speech. Tell everyone what you think.

MAYOR. Kostya, what the hell's wrong with him?

CROWD. He's drunk!

MAYOR. Is he drunk? From one shot?

SERGEY. Ilya – read the speech. The mastodon, remember – you can save us all!

Pause. ILYA *is looking at* NATASHA *again.*

ILYA *deliberately tears up the three speeches.*

MAYOR. What are you doing?! The speech!!

The MAYOR *scrabbles after the pieces of his speech.* KOTOMTSEV *does likewise.*

KOTOMTSEV. You little shit! I'll make your life a misery for this!

SERGEY *shakes his head.*

SERGEY. Ilya... Ilya...

FIRST ILYA (*calmly*). I knew this was how it was going to end up.

SECOND ILYA (*calmly*). There's no way back after this.

FIRST, SECOND and THIRD ILYAS come up to ILYA and lead him to the railings. They take him by the shoulders and throw him into the CROWD.

The CROWD engulf him, their cheers now manic, crazed, devouring.

KOTOMTSEV and the MAYOR join them, furious. ILYA gets lost amongst them.

On the podium, the AIDE and SERGEY watch. SERGEY looks sad. The AIDE looks slyly satisfied.

Suddenly, the CROWD turns out. They all look like ILYA.

ILYA himself has gone.

Slowly they disperse.

SERGEY *leaves the podium. Lights fade on the* AIDE.

Scene Twenty

BABITSKY'*s flat.* BABITSKY *is there, with a small boy,* IVAN. BABITSKY *looks at* IVAN, *smiling.*

BABITSKY. So, we meet at last.

I'm glad that your mother brought you here. Natasha wants me to teach you. She wants me to teach you just like I used to teach her. (*Laughs.*) Well, I'm not so sure about that.

IVAN *sits on the sofa.*

Now tell me – can you wiggle your ears?

IVAN *shakes his head.*

(*Disappointed.*) No? Your grandfather could and your father could. (*He sighs.*) And so the link between generations was ruptured. Never mind...

You know, when I first met your dad, I thought straight away, this one's going to have a complex life. I say that to all my students – well, I've got to give them some sort of encouragement. But the thing is, most of their faces, it's obvious that their life is going to be completely predictable, that... (*He sighs.*) Why am I telling you all this?

IVAN *shrugs his shoulders.*

No, I don't know, either. You know, today, I felt particularly sad. All this morning, I was thinking about your dad, your mum, remembering the whole class. A teacher shouldn't say things like this, but I'm going to say it anyway – they were my best students. You know, there's plenty of examples, through history, of disciples betraying their teachers. Very few examples of the opposite. Next to none. But – I'm an example of it. I mean, I didn't send them off to the Gulags or anything. No...

It is obvious that BABITSKY *is feeling worse.*

No, but I should have done things differently. You know what the problem was? I wanted them to believe in me; I thought I knew what was best for them. I was so busy preparing them for the future. I didn't realise that the past would take so long to die out.

IVAN *shrugs his shoulders, uncertainly.*

Pause.

You know what I'd like, most of all?

IVAN *shrugs his shoulders uncertainly again.*

To go back to that day. And say just one thing to them. 'Believe no one –

– Only yourself.' Only believe in yourself.

BABITSKY *is getting sicker and sicker.*

You're lucky... you haven't understood a thing I've said...
and you know... I'm really tired...

BABITSKY, *trembling, walks to the bookshelf, takes out a
big atlas, and gives it to* IVAN.

This is the history of the dinosaurs... Have a look at it...
look at what there used to be before, what actually existed
once upon a time... and I'll lie down and have a little sleep.

BABITSKY *feels very bad. He lies down on the floor.*

...I'm so tired... Can you really not wiggle your ears?

IVAN *shakes his head.* BABITSKY *raises himself up from
the floor slightly, with a great effort, looks at* IVAN, *and
bends his head.*

I'll show you how to do it. Your mum's going to come soon
and take you home, okay? But I'll show you. Look... Can
you see?

BABITSKY *bends his head and wiggles his ears. Then he
slumps onto the floor.* IVAN *smiles.*

In the town square, a statue of ILYA *stands.*

Blackout.

The End.